A HISTORY

of

BRIDGETOWN CEMETERY

*Quietly Serving
Cincinnati's Western Hills
for over 150 Years*

Joe Flickinger

HERITAGE BOOKS
2021

HERITAGE BOOKS

AN IMPRINT OF HERITAGE BOOKS, INC.

Books, CDs, and more—Worldwide

For our listing of thousands of titles see our website
at
www.HeritageBooks.com

Published 2021 by
HERITAGE BOOKS, INC.
Publishing Division
5810 Ruatan Street
Berwyn Heights, Md. 20740

Heritage Books by the author:

A Bicentennial History of Green Township:
Uncovering a Jewel in the Crown of the Queen City, 1809–2009

A History of Bridgetown Cemetery: Quietly Serving
Cincinnati's Western Hills for over 150 Years

A History of Colerain Township: From Frontier Wilderness to Suburban Sprawl

Cover Photo: Historic Receiving Vault, located in original
sections of cemetery, facing the front of the building.
Photo courtesy of Joe Flickinger

International Standard Book Number
Paperbound: 978-1-55613-423-4

Dedication

This book is dedicated to the many people whose lives intersect at 20 or so acres in Green Township. Your life stories made this book possible.

Table of Contents

List of Illustrations

Foreword

Bridgetown Cemetery was established as the First German Protestant Cemetery of Green Township in 1864. The cemetery is located in Western Hamilton County and celebrated its 150th year of operation in 2014 — its sesquicentennial. The Green Township of 1864 is very different than the one that currently exists. Today the township is a sprawling suburb of Cincinnati, full of housing subdivisions, many stores, numerous cars, and over 60,000 people. In 1864, the township was rural, where farms and livestock outnumbered people well into the early 1920's.

In Joe Flickinger's book, *A History of Bridgetown Cemetery: Quietly Serving Cincinnati's Western Hills for over 150 Years*, you will learn about not only the history and growth of the cemetery from a small, 7 acre cemetery, to the 22 acre community cemetery of today. You will also learn about many points of interest in the original and expanded sections of the cemetery. The two tours in this book provide not only interesting facts and figures relating the cemetery's growth and change over time, but interesting descriptions of symbols found in the cemetery's original sections and areas of future growth in the newest sections as yet to open.

Interesting photos from the cemetery's past, as well as donated photos from the families of the figures who shaped the cemetery over the years are found in this book. One of the most fascinating points of interest is the site of the Green Township Cemetery from Harrison Avenue that was moved to Bridgetown Cemetery in 1975. Many do not know the history of this often-forgotten graveyard, which dates to the establishment of Green Township. This book brings the history of this cemetery back to public awareness. This book brings this history, as well as many other cemetery related stories from Green Township, Cheviot, and other western Hamilton County communities to life.

Bridgetown Cemetery's Board of Trustees were happy to assist Joe in his efforts to publish our history. As a Green Township native and former cemetery groundskeeper from his days in high school and college, Joe has always worked hard to take care of the cemetery and its image. This book is no different. Joe has taken many hours of care to craft our long history into an easy to read book. Today, Joe is a successful history teacher, and local historian. We are proud to showcase our cemetery as the subject of one of his books. Enjoy reading about the story of our 22 acres of Green Township and its history.

Bridgetown Cemetery Trustees
William Flickinger - President
Ron Scheidt - Vice President
Mary Scheidt - Secretary/Treasurer
Nikolaus Gemmell
Daniel Herzog

Acknowledgements

I would like to thank Bridgetown Cemetery and their trustees for their assistance in writing this book. Thank you to everyone who submitted pictures and anecdotes. To my former students, who took my Local History elective, and encouraged me to write books on local history: without your support and encouragement, I would never have tried to write, much less consider researching a topic as big as this book. To Dr. Paul Simon, your willingness to support a small independent study on this cemetery helped me open quite a few doors — thank you! To Dr. Suzie Chung, thank you for the encouragement you gave when writing the basis for this book, my master's thesis. To my parents, William and Nancy Flickinger, who passed their love of books, and writing on to me, I hope this book continues to make you very proud. Without you choosing that house on Weirman Ave, I might not have looked at cemeteries the way I do. I would also like to thank Dan Herzog, Jeff Dreigon, Lou Stroschen, Herman "Bud" Morretta, Verna Carney, Stanley Stall, Ron Scheidt, Judy Boeshart, Mary Schedit, The Menz/Morretta Family, Barbara Semona, Traci Scholtes, Julie Carpenter and Paul Ruffing, for their help and assistance with writing this book. Finally, to my wife Kathleen and children Erin, Ryan, and Kelsey; thank you for putting up with my unending fascination and interest in local history.

Introduction

Bridgetown Cemetery has always held a special place in my own memories. My parents bought a house on Weirman Avenue in October 1978 where the backyard bordered an open field of Bridgetown Cemetery. I was born less than two months later. My earliest memories center around watching the workers of the cemetery cutting the grass, tending to the flower beds, driving and using all kinds of equipment, as well as working funerals. My parents received strange looks from visitors to our home when I played "cemetery man" in my bedroom or in the basement, riding tricycles pretending to cut the grass, or hooking up wagons to those same tricycles and pretending to "dig" graves. While this was strange to some, it was very normal as this is what I observed as a youth during the week. It was a part of daily life I observed from my backyard or back windows. Later memories involve taking walks along the roads with my grandfather and parents, always fascinated with the headstones, both large and small. My imagination was captured by the names carved on those stones, wondering who those people were and what their stories were as well as why some stones were written in a strange language. Finally, I learned how to ride a bike on the quiet roads in the evening with my parents and siblings. My dad would become acquainted with the workers and supervisors and I tagged along when my dad talked to the guys. The talks centered around the neighborhood happenings and updates on projects they were working on in the cemetery. When I was 14, my family moved to a different neighborhood to a house with more room. Little did I know but when I turned sixteen, I was offered a job as a seasonal worker at the same cemetery. I learned the qualities of hard work, modesty, and being able to listen to directions and think on my toes while trimming around headstones with gas powered trimmers, cutting with riding mowers, and helping direct traffic when funerals came to the cemetery. In college, I was given more responsibility, working full time when not in classes throughout the growing seasons, and staying for limited hours in the winter months, and finding out just how quiet an administration building can be during the winter when there is four inches of snow on the ground and the roads have been plowed and salted! It was in college I was given the opportunity to research and write the previously unwritten history of the cemetery as an independent research project for my Bachelor's in History. After graduation, and several years after beginning my professional career as a history teacher, I found my way back into local history and wrote my first book on Green Township history. I also discovered the Green Township Historical Association, where I currently serve as Vice-President.

Bridgetown Cemetery was established in 1864 as the First German Protestant Cemetery Association of Green Township. As the number of burials in the cemetery grew, so did the acreage. In 1937, the cemetery trustees purchased 12.7 acres of adjacent land directly to the north to expand the cemetery to its current twenty-two acre size. After WWII, the cemetery developed this land to mimic the quickly suburbanizing area of Green Township and Bridgetown. Family lots and large, ten foot high headstones were left to the original sections, and the new sections saw straight rows, rigid height restrictions on headstones, and community monuments and gardens with landscaping, mimicking the changing tastes of the community surrounding the cemetery after WWII. This change in culture in both the cemetery and surrounding community will be shown using the archives of the cemetery and two walking tours, one showcasing the original cemetery and its unique features, and the other showing the new sections and how different the appearance is of the layout of the cemetery. I hope you enjoy this book as much as I did while researching and writing it.

Chapter One:
Green Township's Early History and First Cemeteries

Bridgetown Cemetery is located in Bridgetown, a suburb of Green Township, Hamilton County, Ohio. Inhabitants of Green Township and its encompassing communities are very familiar with the area, but many native Cincinnatians are unfamiliar with the western side of Cincinnati. Green Township, as native Cincinnatians know it, can be a puzzle to many "outsiders" because of its unique closeness and its small-town feel within ten miles of a major Midwestern city. Many outsiders venture into Green Township to visit friends and relatives, or attend community events, and emerge surprised and bewildered by the unique names of streets, neighborhoods, and community institutions. The Green Township of today bears little resemblance to the Green Township of pioneer days when Native Americans considered this area their "sacred hunting ground." The Green Township of pioneer days was frontier land, far removed from the small settlement known to many as Losantiville (Cincinnati today). Green Township was dotted with beautiful trickling streams abundant with many types of fish and lands filled with other wildlife such as deer, rabbits, and the occasional bear or two. The Green Township of the late 1700s also had lush, thick forests, making travel through the area by wagon almost impossible unless travelers followed Native American trails. Travel on foot or horseback was an absolute necessity, as many of these trails were less than five feet wide, making settlement in the area very, very slow.

To understand settlement patterns of Green Township, one must follow many of the obstacles in the way of the early settlers of the area. The Native Americans in the area, the Shawnee, were very hostile towards American settlement in the land north of the Ohio River as they considered the Ohio Country as their "sacred hunting ground." At first, many American hunters and trappers navigated their way through the area and made positive contact with the Shawnee and other tribes living in the Ohio Country.

These hunters and trappers hunted for a few months, bartered and traded with the local tribes, and moved on in short order. This contact occurred until the end of the American Revolution when the Proclamation of 1763 was repealed; the settlement opened to just about anyone who wished to move to the newly opened "wild west." The Proclamation of 1763 forbade any further settlement into the Ohio territory by British subjects. This treaty did not stop some of the travelers. The idea of making a fresh start lured individuals to this new "wild west", creating a new beginning where they could make a substantial change in their lives. Despite the Proclamation of 1763, settlement increased, with many individuals choosing the Ohio Valley as an excellent place to start a new life. Many of these settlers were native Virginians; by settling in the Ohio Valley, they chose to stay Virginians because Virginia had claimed a large chunk of the territory. Many of the Virginians who moved here believed that the British Royal agents who oversaw Virginia were not going to pay attention to the movement. This inattention was, in large part, due to the significant distance between the main urban areas of eastern Virginia and the Ohio territory.

During the American Revolution, the Ohio Territory became an area of contention for both colonists and Native Americans. Some settlers saw the region as a bastion of opportunity that was theirs for the taking. Many Native Americans felt deceived by the breaking of the Proclamation of 1763 by the American colonists. Soon the Native Americans became very sympathetic towards the British cause. Many Native Americans saw the vast, stretches of land that they considered their sacred hunting ground being destroyed by the methods used by the new eastern transplants to establish their homes. These Native Americans witnessed land they had farmed, hunted on, and lived within for centuries changed forever by the new settlers. Colonists stripped the land, showing little to no regard for the surrounding environment.
Trees that were hundreds of years old quickly disappeared and the new settlers replaced them with open fields. By the end of the American Revolution, Green Township was still an untamed wilderness, but things were about to change. While the founding fathers were meeting back east to create a new American Government, a few pioneers were making their way to the Ohio Territory utilizing the Cumberland Gap and the newly organized territory of Kentucky. Word began to trickle back east about the beauty and abundance of the Ohio Country. One of these individuals who heard of the potential for growth and profit was a man named Benjamin Stites. Stites made several trips into the area, and

decided to enlist the help of others in his quest to settle and profit from this "wild west."

An essential individual to the history of Green Township, who was also synonymous with the settlement of Cincinnati, was John Cleves Symmes. Symmes was a delegate to the Continental Congress and judge from New Jersey in 1788 when he acquired over 311,000 acres from Congress.[1] In November of that year, a contemporary of Symmes named Benjamin Stites and a small group of settlers made their way down the Ohio River on flatboats and settled in what is today the eastern suburb of Cincinnati named Columbia-Tusculum. Stites and his settlers named their settlement Columbia. In December of that year, Robert Patterson and Mathias Denman led the second group of settlers down the Ohio River. They landed at what is now the Public Landing area of the riverfront of Cincinnati. They named their tiny settlement Losantiville. In 1789, Symmes himself made his way down the river with the third group of settlers and landed west of the Losantiville site, and Symmes named his settlement North Bend, for the steep northern bend the river takes on its way west to the Mississippi River. [2]

Settlement was slow in the territory known as the Northwest Territory, of which Ohio was part of, due in part to the hostile actions taken toward American settlers by the native tribes in the area. In 1790, due to increasing fears of the Shawnee tribes, President George Washington directed the

---

[1] Silberstein, Iola, *Cincinnati, Then and Now*, Cincinnati, League of Women Voters, 1982 10.
[2] Silberstein, 9-10

United States Army to erect a fort for the protection of U.S. citizens settling the area. Settlers built Ft. Washington to hold over 200 troops and serve as a warning to all native tribes considering attacks. Due to the presence of the fort, the settlement remained along the riverfront. Settlers stayed there after a pioneer outpost called Fort Dunlap (in what would later be named Colerain Township) was attacked near the Great Miami River in January 1791. Shawnee forces led by Simon Girty and reportedly Blue Jacket, numbering over 300, surrounded and laid siege to the fort, which was defended by federal soldiers and an officer from Ft. Washington.[3]

Green Township Established

Before Green Township was able to support permanent settlers, the Congress of the United States set up rules for governing and dividing what people called public lands. The Land Ordinance of 1785 created the guidelines for the shape and character of what became Green Township. According to the Land Ordinance, the land was to be divided into six-mile, square townships created by lines running north and south and intersecting at right angles with east/west lines. Townships were to be arranged in north/south rows called ranges. Most townships were to be subdivided into 36 one-mile square sections. Each range, township, and section were to be numbered in a regular, consistent

---

[3] Kramb, Edwin A. *Buckeye battlefields*. Springboro, OH: Valhalla Press, 2006.

sequence. [4] Unlike most of Ohio, the Symmes Purchase was a mixture of townships divided in different directions. Some are laid out in east to west fashion. These are called fractional ranges.

In 1788 the Symmes purchase was settled and split into three distinct townships: Columbia, Losantiville, and Miami. These townships were three vast areas encompassing almost all of what is now modern Hamilton County. These three areas were formed from the three original settlements of the Symmes Purchase. These three areas were: Columbia, settled by Benjamin Stites in November 1788; Losantiville, settled in late December 1788, and North Bend, established by John Cleves Symmes in 1789. The Green Township we know of today had its roots in portions of the original Miami and Losantiville townships. Losantiville became known as Cincinnati Township after the Governor of the Northwest Territory, Arthur St. Claire, visited Losantiville and renamed it Cincinnati. Another reason for St. Claire's visit was the establishment of a county, which they named Hamilton, in honor of the current Treasury Secretary and Revolutionary War hero, Alexander Hamilton. In 1795, Timothy Symmes, who was the only full brother of John Cleves Symmes, established South bend Township to accommodate South Bend, the brand new settlement close to what is now Anderson Ferry. John Cleves Symmes touted North Bend as the future home of the metropolis of his purchased lands, because of its

---

[4] Knepper, Dr. George, *The Official Ohio Lands Book* , Columbus Ohio, Auditor of the State of Ohio Publication, 2002, 13-16

central location. This idea was supported by a detachment of 21 federal troops stationed there for a short time before the establishment of Fort Washington. Unfortunately, the area grew undesirable when floodwaters forced the abandonment of the settlement to higher ground. Much of the Symmes Purchase remained loosely organized, massive townships, while most of the attention for settlement was given to Cincinnati after the establishment of Ft. Washington. South Bend Township included all of today's Delhi Township and most of Green Township.

Colerain Township claimed small sections of today's northern Green Township, which was formed in 1794 by the Court of General Quarter Sessions of Peace. In 1803, Ohio became the 17th state, changing the civil divisions. This is when sources indicate that Hamilton County began to shrink, as many newer counties were formed from Hamilton County. These newer counties included Butler and Warren counties to the north and Clermont County to the east. Hamilton County came very close to the shape it is today. From this point, surveyors began carving up Hamilton County into the different townships as outlined in the Land Ordinance of 1785. Green Township, labeled within the Symmes Purchase as Fractional Range 2, Township 2, was the only township created in the Symmes Purchase that was a total of 36 square miles. The accepted date of creation for Green Township is 1809.

While no known account exists of the first trustees or their meetings, an early source describes the early government structure of beginning of the townships in Hamilton County. The state law stipulated that once a suitable amount of men wanted to establish a government, the County Constable must call a meeting, and he helped choose a presiding officer of the meeting. He was given orders to arrest anyone who disturbed the meeting. Fifteen male taxpayers had to be present, and they, in turn, elected officials by secret ballot. These officials consisted of three or more trustees, two overseers of the poor, three fence viewers, two appraisers of houses, one lister of property, and many supervisors of land. In the early history of the township, it was not considered an honor to hold office; pay was low, resources were not readily available, and guidance from state officials was non-existent. Due to these conditions, after being elected to office, anyone refusing was fined $5. By 1831 it was reduced to a fine of $2. After 1850, the offices paid too much to be rejected.[5]

Today, the Green Township slate of elected officials consists of three township trustees and a fiscal officer. They all run for office using modern political campaigns and township residents vote for candidates who are at least 18 years old and registered to vote. The trustees vote upon any other positions within the township administration, and many of the jobs, including the police and fire departments, use civil service examinations to produce the best and brightest candidates for possible approval by the township trustees.[6]

---

[5] Scully, Henry, ed, *Remember When...Monfort Heights*, Cincinnati Ohio, Monfort Heights Civic Association, 1977, 19
[6] Green Township Webpage, (accessed 4/29/2020) http://www.greentwp.org

Earliest Cemeteries

The earliest cemeteries in Green Township were most often family graveyards. Many were set off to one section of early township farms, and after many generations were often forgotten as the wooden or sandstone headstones weathered away by the elements. The first organized cemeteries were not established until the 1820s. While some may have been developed earlier, it is nearly impossible to ascertain through records from the time if this is the case. These early cemeteries were religious centered, often close to a church and restricted to members of the congregation. The other option was public cemeteries, which were smaller, and had little to no money for upkeep.

Possibly the earliest cemetery in Green Township was the Township Cemetery, originally located along Harrison Ave in the current City of Cheviot. Much debate today exists between local historians as to how early this cemetery was established in Green Township. The actual documentation from the establishment of this cemetery may never be found. Although one interpretation states that in 1809, after the establishment of Green Township, the Burnet, Findlay, & Harrison Land Company set aside this plot of land to Green Township for use as a public cemetery and a meeting house/religious building, no firm documentation exists to back up this claim. Pioneers of all faiths were buried in this cemetery through the years this cemetery was active; the earliest documented burial being possibly in 1812.[7] A meeting house/religious building on the site was made of logs, and it was supposedly destroyed by a falling tree in 1816.[8] This cemetery has been called the "township cemetery," and often just the "Green Township Cemetery."[9] Sometime in 1822, the Bethel Baptist church acquired the deed to the cemetery and expanded it further south.[10] Many pioneers from early Green Township and Cheviot history are buried here, including Craigs, Johnsons, & Hildreth's, as well as Thomas Egan, Green Townships only casualty from the Mexican War in 1846.[11] The last recorded burial in this small cemetery was in 1920.[12] In 1954, the cemetery fell into disrepair, with many of the old headstones damaged by time and neglect. The Bethel Baptist, since renamed Westwood Baptist Church, leased the cemetery land to Cheviot. Cheviot had the headstones removed and stored nearby with a single headstone dedicated to the memory of the pioneers buried here. The back half of the land without

---

[7] Looker Palmer & Reynolds, ed., "On Tuesday Last," *Liberty Hall* (Cincinnati, December 22, 1812), sec. 1, p. 1.

[8] Alexander Long, "Green Township History for Harvest Home Picnic," *Cincinnati Daily Enquirer* (Cincinnati, August 27, 1869).

[9] Mary H Remler, ed., *Hamilton County, Ohio Burial Records Green Township*, vol. 10 (Westminster, Maryland: Heritage Books, 2012), 90

[10] *Deed Book of Hamilton County, Deed Book of Hamilton County*, vol. 145 (Cincinnati, OH, n.d.), p. 106.

[11] William Heglin, "Honor to the Dead," *The Cincinnati Daily Enquirer* (Cincinnati, July 3, 1847).

[12] Remler, 90

burials was used for parking.[13] In early 1975, Cheviot purchased the property from the church. To better honor the lives and memories of the pioneers buried here, Cheviot paid to have the graves and any remnants of headstones moved to Bridgetown Cemetery by the end of June 1975.[14] A single marker sits on top of the moved cemetery dedicated to the pioneers of Green Township. In 1976, Cheviot dedicated a small patriot park and expanded the parking area on the spot of the recently moved cemetery.

The township cemetery is often connected to another religious cemetery located just north of and directly across Harrison Ave, the Bethel Baptist Cemetery. Historic accounts connect the two cemeteries as early as 1822. However, no firm records survive which show when Bethel Cemetery had its first burials, nor do they indicate if the Township and Bethel burial grounds were officially operated as separate burial places .[15] The Bethel Baptist Cemetery was deeded to the City of Cheviot and was completely restored thanks to a Boy Scout Project in 2009. Today, the City of Cheviot maintains the old Bethel Church/Westwood Baptist cemetery on the north side of Harrison Ave.[16]

---

[13] Remler, 90

[14] Suburban Topics, ed., "Bulldozer Unearths Casket," *Cincinnati Enquirer* (Cincinnati, May 16, 1975), sec. Metro Section, p. 39.

[15] Marie Dickore, "The Cheviot, Ohio Cemetery," *Bulletin of the Historical and Philosophical Society of Ohio*, 1st ser., 14 (January 1956).

[16] Shauna Steigerwald, "Scout Spruces up Cemetery for Eagle Project," *Cincinnati Enquirer* (Cincinnati, June 6, 2009), sec. Hometown Section, p. 108.

An early religious cemetery established in Green Township was the cemetery located adjacent to the old Ebenezer Methodist Church at the "old five-way" intersection of Cleves Pike(today's Bridgetown Road), Ebenezer Road, and Miamitown Road(today's Taylor Road). This church had a deed recorded at the courthouse in April 1816, with what appears to be the earliest verified burial in 1821. This initial date was identified through gravestone readings in the early 1980s.[17]

Another early religious cemetery in Green Township includes the Asbury Methodist Cemetery, located on West Fork Road in Monfort Heights. The church dates to as early as 1826, with the earliest verified date a burial that took place in 1839.[18] Another old cemetery includes the Roman Catholic St. James Church Cemetery located in White Oak in the northern section of Green Township, which dates its first burial to 1841. St. James is still an active cemetery in Green Township.[19] Roman Catholics in the southern portion of Green Township also have St Aloysius Gonzaga Cemetery, located behind the present church. The cemetery was laid out in 1868, with the first burial occurring in November of that year. It is still an active cemetery in Green Township.[20] The United Brethren Cemetery, also on

[17] Mary H Remler, ed., *Hamilton County, Ohio Burial Records Green Township*, vol. 10 (Westminster, Maryland: Heritage Books, 2012), 94.
[18] Remler, 155
[19] Remler, 157
[20] Paul Ruffing, *St. Aloysius Gonzaga 150th Anniversary Booklet, 1866-2016* (Cincinnati, Ohio: St. Aloysius Gonzaga Church, 2016), 6.

West Fork Road, was established in 1847, with the earliest verified burial in 1849. Many early German pioneers to Green Township who belonged to this church are buried here. This Cemetery is maintained today by Green Township.[21]

Several family cemeteries still exist in Green Township as well. The Lingo Cemetery, located on North Bend Road, was established in 1847 by Obediah Lingo for family and friends. Obediah Lingo owned and operated a sawmill and owned a large tract of land. Members of the Lingo family, as well as friends of the family, are buried in this one-acre cemetery.[22]

The Markland Family Cemetery still exists on the Hollmeyer Orchard land at the south side of Fiddlers Green Road. It was established in 1848 on six-hundredths of an acre of land. Several headstones are still in existence.[23]

Finally, the Van Blaricum Cemetery remains on private property on the west side of Van Blaricum Road about one mile south of South Road. This Cemetery was established in 1865 on one acre of land on what was at the time the Van Blaricum farm. According to gravestone readings, the last burial to occur here was in 1928.[24] Several sources also list this cemetery as the Muddy Creek Cemetery.

"So what was on the land before it became a cemetery?"

---

[21] Remler, 88
[22] Remler, 86
[23] Remler, 154
[24] Remler, 99

Research into deed records shows that the land that is currently the Bridgetown Cemetery was owned by the Findlay, Burnet, and Harrison Company, and subsequently George Torrence, an early Hamilton County Judge and politician, who held the land until he died in 1852. His property was called the George Torrence Estate, and it was split up by his heirs into six parcels. Mr. and Mrs. Martin Smith and Mr.and Mrs. L.B. Dawson owned the original four acres of the cemetery. In June 1864, this group sold to a group of investors made up of George Ahring, J.H. Nagel, Jacob Wuest, and G.W.H Musekamp and their wives. This group ended up selling to the newly organized cemetery association in July 1864.[25] There is currently no documentation of any Native American earthworks, early pioneer activity, or farming on the land.

---

[25] Hamilton County Recorder's Office, Deed Book Document Images, Hamilton County Recorder's Office, Cincinnati., Book 309, 342.

This photograph taken from an airplane sometime in the 1950s shows the Ebenezer graveyard, located at the "old five-way" intersection of Bridgetown, Ebenezer, and Taylor Roads. In 2020, the intersection is now a four-way intersection, with Taylor Road re-routed further west. (Photo courtesy Green Township Historical Association)

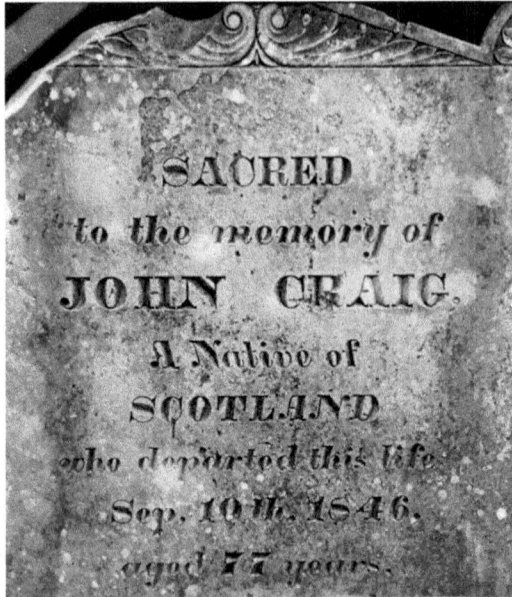

A photograph of the headstone of John Craig, a Green Township settler who is credited with the layout and platting of an early Green Township village, now known as the city of Cheviot, Hamilton County, Ohio. Craig was buried in the old "township cemetery" on the south side of Harrison Ave. Craig's grave, along with all other remains, were moved to Bridgetown Cemetery in 1975 when the church which owned the land could not care for the graves any longer and sold the property to the City of Cheviot. Many of the broken headstones were buried in the mass grave in Bridgetown Cemetery. This headstone was preserved and now resides in the archives of the Cheviot Historical Society. (Photo Courtesy Green Township Historical Association)

[17]

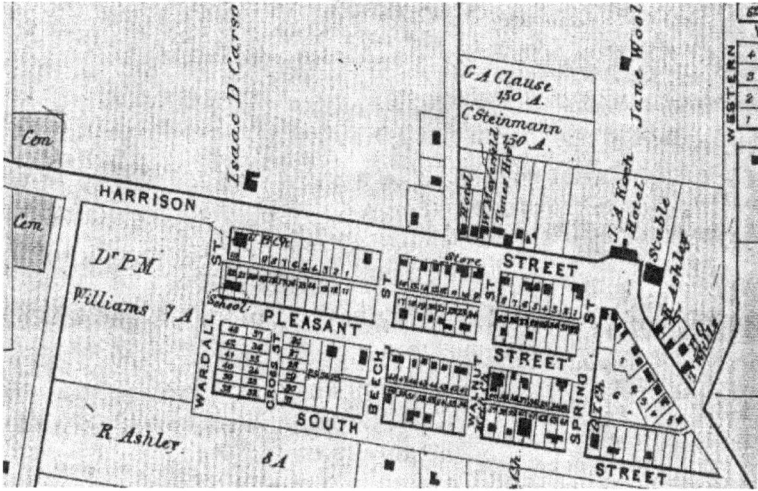

This 1869 map shows the Green Township village of
Cheviot with Harrison Ave running through the
center of the laid-out town. The Bethel and
Township cemeteries are on the upper left side of the
map, facing each other on opposite sides of Harrison
Ave. (Map Courtesy Green Township Historical
Association)

A photograph of the Bethel Cemetery in 2020, which is still in existence in Cheviot on the north side of Harrison Avenue. It was restored thanks to an Eagle Scout Project in 2009 and is currently maintained by the City of Cheviot. This small cemetery is the perfect example of a small community cemetery. (Photo courtesy Joe Flickinger)

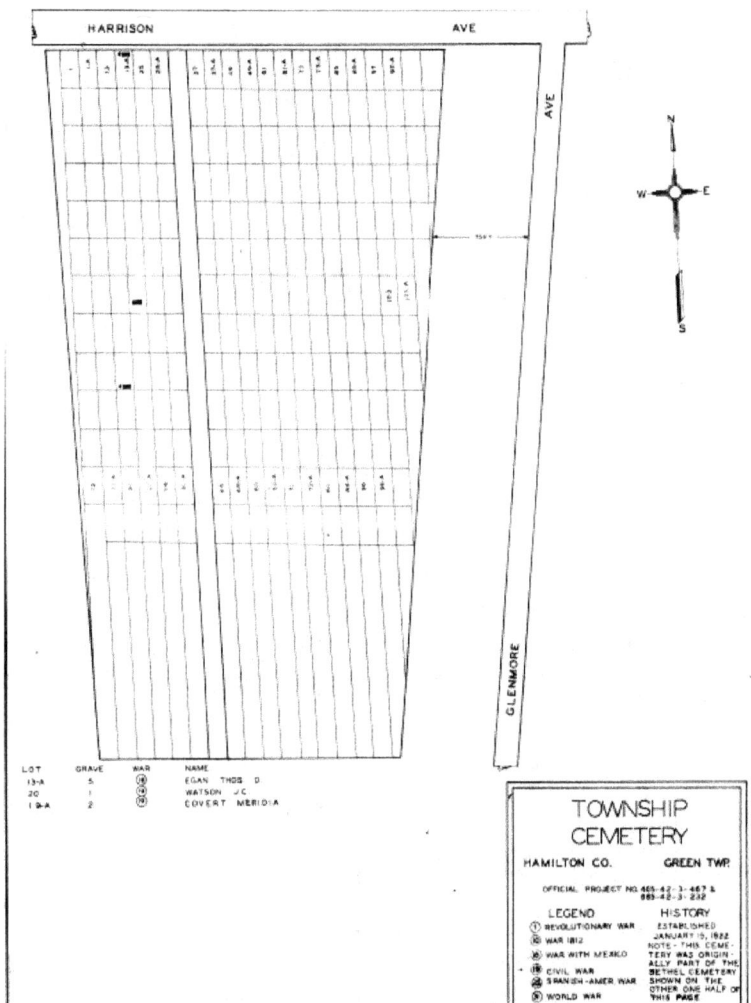

This map is the only known map of veterans who were buried in the "Township" Cemetery on the south side of Harrison Ave. This map was created by the WPA in 1939 and is one of the only maps left which show any burial locations in this early cemetery. (Courtesy Bridgetown Cemetery Association Archive)

[20]

Chapter Two:
A Need for a Place of Their Own

Rural life in Green Township

When settlers arrived, the first task was the establishment of shelter. Since most of the first individuals who made their way to Green Township were the men, a quick lean-to was the cheap and speedy solution to the shelter issue. Families later joined the men after a more permanent shelter was underway or finished. Many of these first cabins were neither fancy nor comfortable. Scores of the early settlers found the fear of Indian attack to be a frightening idea and sought comfort in numbers, so small settlements developed for protection from attack.

Once communities were developed, farmers spent the majority of their first year clearing the land for use as fields to grow their crops. Next was the establishment of a reliable water supply. Countless township creeks and streams provided the water necessary to produce the crops as well as quench the thirst of the growing population. Often the seasons dictated what was grown. Throughout the growing season, farmers raised fruits such as cherries, peaches, apples, and melons, and farmers either sold the produce immediately at one of the many markets in Cincinnati, were consumed by the family, or made into preserves. Vegetables such as cabbage, onions, tomatoes, and various varieties of corn were grown, and farmers either used the food on the farm or sold the crops at the market. In the early days, farmers organized one trip per week to Cincinnati, due to the distance and roads into the city. Sometimes, the overabundance of certain crops would lead to their disposal in the city waterways on their way home. Phillip Steinman III recounted in his book "*Beechwood Flats*" about often having to dump excess crops such as tomatoes into the Mill Creek because everyone had bought their fill. According to Steinman, even the ketchup factories would not take the vegetables, and since they had more than their fair share back on the farm, they would just dump them in the water![26]

By the 1850 census, the United States was a burgeoning country, with the main cities such as New York, Philadelphia, Baltimore, Pittsburgh, and Cincinnati ruling the countryside they straddled. In 1848, a significant revolution in an area of Europe known today as Germany sent a massive influx of German settlers and refugees into the Cincinnati area.[27]

From early on, the number of farms and subsequent little villages began to multiply surrounding Cincinnati. Many small communities were established in rural areas surrounding midwestern cities in order to meet the needs of these new farming residents. Shops catering to the goods and services needed on a farm were common. Add in the 48'ers and the subsequent German immigration,

---

[26] Steinman III, Phillip, *Beechwood Flats*, (New York NY, Vantage Press, 1960) 17

[27] Tolzmann, Don Heinrich, *German Heritage Guide to the Greater Cincinnati Area*, Milford Ohio, Little Miami Publishing, 2003, 13

and you have a recipe for a stable, almost steady population flow to the outlying rural communities of Green Township. The Germans who settled in Cincinnati and its surrounding townships often exemplified the stereotypes held by Americans about Teutonic natives. Many Germans were described as having heavy beards and wearing a different hat than other Americans. These immigrants were highly thought of for their competence in business affairs and frugal natures, which gained the respect of immigrants and native-born Americans all over Cincinnati.[28] Many attribute thrift and ability to the way many of the rural farmers lived. Many were not overly wealthy; they were thrifty and straightforward individuals. Daily rural life was repetitious, and to some, very monotonous. However, this way of life did have some rewards. Many of these farmers made their way to Cincinnati to sell their goods in the many markets throughout the city's neighborhoods. Others loaded up their wagons and ventured into College Hill or Clifton to sell their products. Many farmers drove their cattle, pigs, and other livestock through the muddied roads into the city for the many slaughterhouses that made up a vital piece of the Cincinnati economy in the 1800s. Even though the population of Green Township was small compared to Cincinnati, it was a vital cog in the industrial machine of the city. Life was slow but very rewarding indeed.

Various activities broke up the monotony of the daily grind. One event was the breaking of wild horses that had been delivered to the different

---

[28] Tolzmann, 14

farmers.[29] Another distraction occurred when the wayward traveling salesman was chased up the nearest tree by the family dog. Many families preferred bulldogs or Newfoundlands as the family pets due to their protective nature. These traveling salesmen sold needles, thread, and other various, sundry items that the farms needed but couldn't justify a day's journey into Cincinnati. The salesmen went from farm to farm selling essentials. A revealing fact about the nature of the families and farmers is that they would often invite the salesman to eat with them after calming the upset guard dogs that patrolled these old farms.[30] The farmers and their communities were tightly knit, and the families were even closer. Even though this rural way of life may have given way to suburban developments, the close ties that people feel towards Green Township persist, an authentic connection and pride to the area that many communities of today lack.

As stated before, Green Township had several categories of cemeteries. Public cemeteries such as the Township Cemetery were too small for a growing German population buying up land and establishing roots in the area. Many families deemed Spring Grove Cemetery in Spring Grove Village as too far away for a reasonable visit to deceased family and friends. Roads to and from were dirt or macadam, which made travel in inclement weather by horse or buggy impossible. Other cemeteries were reserved for families or specific religious groups.

---

[29] Steinman, 20
[30] Steinman, 21-22

A plot of land on Cleves Pike was purchased on December 1, 1864, by a group of Protestant landowners in Green Township, Hamilton County, Ohio, as the First German Protestant Cemetery. This land was part of the George Torrence Estate, which was located in section 15 in township two, second fractional range in the Miami Purchase.[31] The deed book of the Hamilton County Recorder's Office shows the names of the first trustees of the cemetery as George H. Aring, Martin Barwick, Gasset Stammel, G.W.H Musekamp, Philip Steinman, and Philip Bayer.[32] The original purchase acreage of the cemetery is today located at 4428 Cincinnati-Cleves Turnpike, now named Bridgetown Road.[33]

In 1871, the cemetery trustees donated a half-acre of land to the First German Protestant Church for the construction of their first church.[34] The original church has been torn down, rebuilt, and renamed as the Pilgrim United Church of Christ in

---

[31] Hamilton County Recorder's Office, Deed Book Document Images, Hamilton County Recorder's Office, Cincinnati., Book 309, 342.

[32] Recorders Deed Book, Book 309, 342.

[33] *Archives of Bridgetown Cemetery Association*, July 2000. Brochure, Formerly Known as The First German Protestant Cemetery of Green Township, Administration Building, Cincinnati.

[34] Hamilton County Recorder's Office, Deed Book Document Images, Hamilton County Recorder's Office, Cincinnati, Book 389, 242.

1961.[35] In 1876, money was raised by cemetery trustees for the construction of a limestone brick receiving vault, for the storing of caskets and bodies temporarily.[36] The cemetery receiving vault looked like a small chapel with two steel doors, and a mantle above the doors with 1877 inscribed. The building was used for the storing of bodies if the weather was too harsh to dig or if the funeral had to be delayed. This building was used for this purpose until the 1920's when local funeral homes were equipped with refrigeration. While the building was used for this purpose, a total of six bodies with caskets were stored in this building for at least several days, from its opening in 1877 to its conversion to a storage building for tools and cemetery supplies in the late 1920s.[37] The Receiving Vault was built by local stonemason and cemetery trustee Phillip Steinman.[38] The Receiving Vault was only to be used from October 1 to May 1, with a $5.00 Deposit that was to be kept by the Cemetery if the storage of a body was to be over two days. If bodies for other cemeteries were to be stored in the building, the cemetery trustees could double the

---

[35] Jeffrey Leuders, *Pilgrim United Church of Christ, 1870-1990* (Cincinnati, OH: Church Printing, 1990).

[36] *Archives of Bridgetown Cemetery Association,* Constitution and Bylaws, 1910.

[37] *Archives of Bridgetown Cemetery Association,* Cemetery Burial Records, 1875-1932.

[38] Phillip Steinman, *Beechwood Flats* (New York: Vantage Press, 1960), 11.

price for the use of the building.[39] In 1880, a bell was commissioned from the Buckeye Bell Company in Cincinnati, Ohio, for a bronze bell to be cast for the bell tower of the cemetery receiving vault.[40] This bell is still housed in the receiving vault, and can still be rung.

In April 1897, the trustees of the cemetery filed Articles of Incorporation with the Secretary of State of the State of Ohio, Charles Kinney. These articles were renewed until the cemetery expanded and renamed in 1961.[41] Streetcars were extended to the Cincinnati neighborhood of Westwood in 1898, which is located on the eastern border of the Green Township village of Cheviot.[42] This helped grow the population of Green Township, which increased the number of burials in the cemetery. The cemetery board of trustees began investigating how to increase the size of the cemetery around the 1920's.

Trustee meeting minutes express an interest in property located directly northwest of the original cemetery property owned by the Aring family. The

---

[39] *Archives of Bridgetown Cemetery Association,* Constitution and Bylaws of the First German Protestant Cemetery Association, 1910.

[40] *Archives of Bridgetown Cemetery Association.* Trustee Meeting minutes, 1938-1961.

[41] *Archives of Bridgetown Cemetery Association.* Article of Incorporation, 1897.

[42] Joe Flickinger, *A Bicentennial History of Green Township: Uncovering a Jewel in the Crown of the Queen City; 1809-2009* (Westminster, Maryland: Heritage Books, 2011), 56.

[28]

Bridgetown School District considered buying this property for their new school. The cemetery board decided to back off the cemetery interest in this land due to the school district's enthusiasm for a new school building to replace the 1878 building that was currently in use. This land eventually became the site of the new Bridgetown School in 1939.

In 1932, the cemetery board of trustees started negotiations with two property owners adjoining the cemetery directly to the north and west. The Schaperklaus family farm directly to the north was interested in selling their 12.7-acre farm to the cemetery. In 1939, the cemetery bought the property from the Schaeperklaus family for the expansion of the cemetery for $14,732.[43] In 1960, the cemetery board of trustees hired a full-time cemetery superintendent. The position was also referred to as a cemeterian in the board of trustee minutes. The job had the responsibility of hiring employees when needed for grounds work, ordering supplies, performing maintenance on the cemetery equipment, and being on call for grave sales, funeral planning, and for burials. The position would answer directly to the cemetery board.[44]

In 1961, with the development of the new land almost complete, the cemetery board held an opening ceremony on Sunday, October 1, 1961, at the nearly completed administration building. The ceremony

---

[43] *Archives of Bridgetown Cemetery Association*, Board of Trustees Minute Book, 1938-1961.

[44] *Archives of Bridgetown Cemetery Association*, Board of Trustees Minute Book, 1938-1961.

included speeches from a cemetery trustee, several ministers from local churches, and singing from the Syrian Shrine Chanters. It was at this ceremony that the name officially became Bridgetown Cemetery. This change in name was meant to reflect the non-denominational shift for the Cemetery as well. As the community became more diverse, the board of trustees expanded burial access beyond Protestant Germans to include any resident of Green Township and surrounding communities.[45]

In 1962, the cemetery board opened its administration building and moved all trustee meetings to the cemetery administration building in 1964. The opening of the new building was also a change from the past as well. Meetings were traditionally held in the Sunday School Room of the First German Protestant Church since the cemetery donated the land to the church in the early 1870s. Now meetings could be held in the cemetery's building without paying a fee for the use of another building. The board authorized an addition to the new building when they discovered it was too small for the equipment owned by the cemetery.[46] The 1970s and 1980s saw increased sales and burials in Bridgetown Cemetery as the surrounding areas began to transition from farm fields to subdivisions. After several decades of interments numbering

---

[45] *Archives of Bridgetown Cemetery Association,* Cemetery Dedication and Consecration Program.

[46] *Archives of Bridgetown Cemetery Association,* Board of Trustees Minute Book, 1961-1995.

between fifty and sixty burials, 1973 experienced the most significant jump in funerals, from fifty-two burials in 1972 to eighty-one burials in 1973.[47] This trend would continue into the early 2000s.

In 1985, several part-time employees were hired by the cemetery for twelve-month periods, in addition to the full-time grounds superintendent. They worked forty plus hours from March to October and less than ten hours weekly from November to February. These employees would help with burials during the winter months, and any other maintenance needs the cemetery had, which included snow removal and equipment maintenance.[48] The cemetery purchased a John Deere backhoe in January 1995 so cemetery employees could dig graves, eliminating the need for an outside contractor. The cemetery also invested in zero-turn mowers to allow for quicker mowing to be completed by cemetery employees.[49] In 2017, a new section was laid out in response to a growing number of burials of cremated remains. This new section features smaller lots that can accommodate two cremated remains in a concrete vault.[50] Bridgetown Cemetery today averages around 50-60 burials per

[47] *Archives of Bridgetown Cemetery Association,* Cemetery Burial Records, 1965-1978.

[48] *Archives of Bridgetown Cemetery Association,* Board of Trustees Minute Book, 1961-1995.

[49] *Archives of Bridgetown Cemetery Association,* Board of Trustees Minute Book, 1961-1995.

[50] *Archives of Bridgetown Cemetery Association,* Board of Trustees Minute Book, 1998-present.

year. Cremation burials continue to rise in the 21st century, yet pre-paid burial lots have declined, so the cemetery projects they will have enough space for the next 50-75 years.

Verfassung

des

Ersten Deutschen
Protestantischen

Kirchhof = Vereins

von

Green Township

◻▷◁◻

Cincinnati, Ohio
Chas. J. Lotz Printing & Stationery Co.
1910

The title page from the 1910 rules book from the cemetery translates as "The Constitution of the First German Protestant Cemetery Association of Green Township." The book was printed in a German script called "Kurrent." It also has a second part of the book written in English. Many other cemetery records were handwritten in this German Script until 1920. (Bridgetown Cemetery Archives)

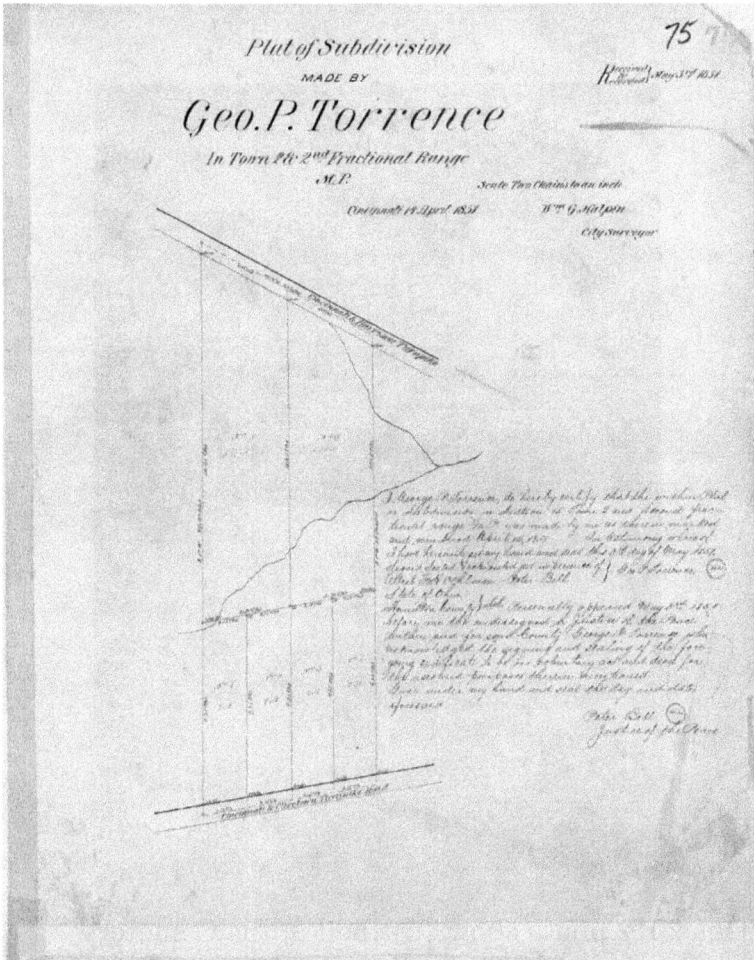

The plat map of the George Torrence Subdivision shows the cemetery as it would have appeared in 1852 when the property was divided and sold. Notice the tributary creek, which is drawn through the middle of the land. This would be troublesome

for the expansion of the cemetery until the early
1960s. (Bridgetown Cemetery Archives)

This 2012 photo shows the bell in the Cemetery
receiving vault. The bell was installed in 1880 from
the Buckeye Bell Company. It was rung for funerals
as they entered the cemetery until the early 1910's.
(Photo courtesy Ed and Dan Herzog)

Chapter Three:
Original Cemetery Points of Interest

This chapter is the first of a two-part walking tour of Bridgetown Cemetery comprised of 14 "stops" along the older sections of the cemetery. Graves of prominent individuals in the cemetery and surrounding community are highlighted. The principal stop on this section of the tour is the cemetery receiving vault. It was built in 1876-1877 to hold bodies and caskets of the deceased when a grave could not be dug during harsh or cold weather. This brick building located close to the back of the original cemetery houses a bell dated 1880, which can still be rung in its steeple, and features steel doors.

The tour features several headstones that are unique in funerary art including the large obelisks that are present in the cemetery and the use of symbols on headstones, like willow trees, an urn draped in a veil, and a tombstone shaped like a tree stump. Some of these show the veil between heaven and earth, others symbolized everlasting life, or a life cut short. Pilgrim United Church of Christ, located next to the original cemetery sections, is highlighted as well since many of the early members of this church are buried in the original parts of the cemetery. An interesting fact mentioned is that the cemetery donated the half acre of land where the original church building was situated.

The second tour focuses on the newer sections of the cemetery, which were bought in 1939 as the population of Green Township grew. The opening of these sections in 1961 attracted increased growth to the cemetery. Remains from several small graveyards in Green Township were reinterred in the new sections. The stops on the second tour include the cemetery administration building, reinterments from two smaller cemeteries, landscaped contemplative areas, and several areas designated for individual burials. This tour focuses less on stories of people to explore the growth and infrastructure that the cemetery experienced after WWII in opening the newly acquired sections.

Several points of interest have been chosen to highlight the history of the original sections of the cemetery to the area. As the newer parts of the cemetery continues to hold burials, efforts have been made to respect the privacy of those who have recently passed and their families. Using this book as a reference, you may take a self-guided tour at your own pace. Please be aware of traffic on cemetery roads, while traffic has a set speed limit of 5 mph, sometimes drivers may be inattentive, and may not pay close enough attention rounding bends in the road or see walkers on the cemetery roads. Please be respectful of mourners and avoid walking in areas where someone is visiting the grave of a loved one out of respect for that person's privacy. When walking in the older sections, please be aware that the ground is not level, and unseen dips in the ground may be present, which may cause tripping hazards and could cause injury. Do not make rubbings on older headstones; these headstones, often made from a porous stone, have become brittle over time, and are easily damaged by rubbings. Please park along the side of the roads, or in any marked parking spots.

Tour #1: Original Cemetery

Begin at the Bridgetown Road entrance. Established in 1864 as the First German Protestant Cemetery, it was also known as Bridgetown Protestant Cemetery. Unless otherwise noted, information is obtained from the trustee minutes and archives of the Bridgetown Cemetery Association.

Original cemetery points of interest. Begin at entrance off of Bridgetown Road. Points of interest begin at #1.

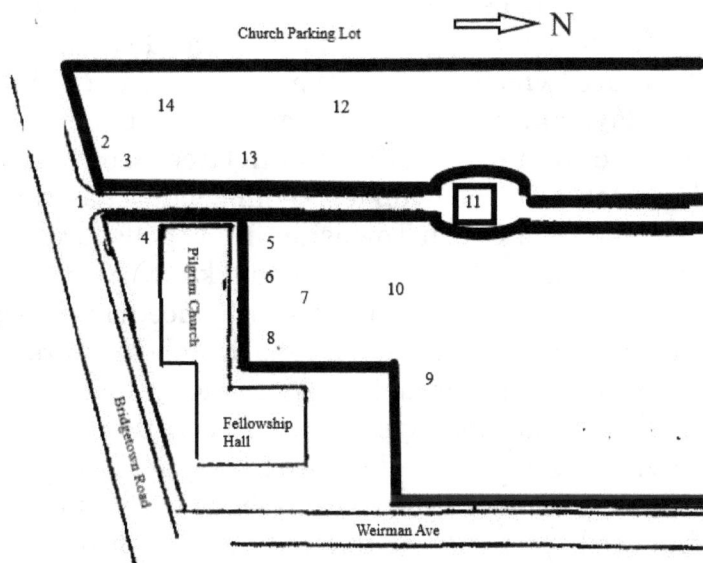

Stop #1

Your tour begins at the original entrance to the cemetery. Purchased in the summer of 1864 by a group of local Protestant landowners, the cemetery was named The First German Protestant Cemetery of Green Township. The land originally was part of an estate owned by Cincinnati Judge George Torrence, who purchased the property from the Findlay, Harrison, and Burnet Land Company, who had acquired most of the land in Green Township from John Cleves Symmes. Symmes purchased much of the area of Green Township from the federal government in what later became known as the Symmes Purchase. This entrance once had a large wooden fence, which had a gate attached. Horse-drawn carriages brought visitors along a macadam road on major holidays such as Decoration Day(Memorial Day today). In later years, the cemetery replaced the wooden fence with an iron fence, which had large iron gates with "Bridgetown Protestant Cemetery" emblazoned on the front.

[41]

These gates were later moved in 1961 to the new Harrison Ave entrance and were attached to the stone pillars built there. Today, this entrance looks out onto busy Bridgetown Road, and borders Pilgrim United Church of Christ, which celebrates the 150th anniversary of its founding in 2021.

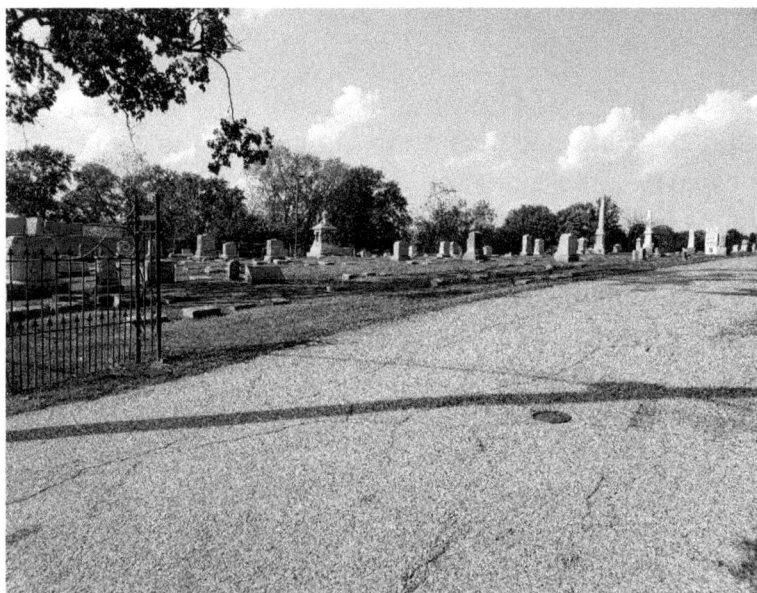

The original entrance of the First German Protestant Cemetery served from 1864 until the newly purchased and developed sections opened in 1961. (Photo Courtesy Joe Flickinger)

Stop #2

This iron fence is another aspect of the Cemetery that has changed over time along with the cemetery property. The fence replaced an old wooden split rail fence that acted as a natural border between Bridgetown Road and the burial sites within the cemetery. The original split rail fence was built after concern in the late 1800s about livestock from farmers wandering from Cleves-Bridgetown Pike(today's Bridgetown Road). Several trustee meetings featured complaints from lot owners that several cows had wandered onto the cemetery property during different parts of the year and were destroying the grass that was growing on the family lots. The cemetery trustees had a wooden split rail fence constructed to address the complaints. In the late 1930s, after the road was paved over with

[43]

asphalt and automobile traffic became a concern, the cemetery board voted to purchase and install the decorative iron fence seen in the picture. This fence would have run along the southern end of the cemetery and wrapped along ten feet north along with the neighboring Hahn property.

The original iron fence installed in the late 1930s

went along the complete southern edge of the property that bordered Bridgetown Road. (Photo courtesy Joe Flickinger)

Stop #3

Just inside the original entrance is the family plot of the Musekamp Family. George H. W. Musekamp was a prominent physician in Green Township, as well as a leading holder of political office. His son, George H Musekamp, was also a doctor who held elected office in Green Township as treasurer. George H. W Musekamp served as a prominent doctor in Green Township and helped establish the First German Protestant Cemetery in 1864. He later helped organize the First German Protestant Church by hosting organizational meetings in his home in Cheviot. He was instrumental in arranging for the cemetery to donate a half-acre of land to the church for the construction of their first building in 1871.

This photo shows the main stone of the Musekamp family plot located directly inside the original entrance to the cemetery. Dr. George H. W. Musekamp was a prominent physician in Green Township. He and several family members held political office in the township government as well. (Photo courtesy Joe Flickinger)

This sketch is a likeness of Dr. George H. W. Musekamp, a prominent Green Township physician and one of the first trustees who established the cemetery in 1864. (Bridgetown Cemetery Archives)

Cheviot, Ohio, Nov. 1, 1911.

Dear Sir:

Having been honored by the Republican Party with the Nomination of Treasurer of Green Township, I desire, by honest endeavor, to be elected. The activity of the campaign may prevent me calling on you personally, so I take this means of advising you of my candidacy and soliciting your vote and assistance.

Very truly yours,

Geo H Musekamp M D

Photo by Macke, Cheviot, Ohio.

This election postcard shows Dr. George H. Musekamp running for Green Township Treasurer in 1911. These types of cards were often sent through the mail, just like today's political cards and literature. George was the son of Dr. George H.W. Musekamp, one of the original trustees and founding members of the cemetery. George H. is also buried in Bridgetown Cemetery, but in a different family lot. (Courtesy Green Township Historical Association)

Stop #4

Pilgrim United Church of Christ (originally named The First German Protestant Church of Green Township) was established in August 1870 after a meeting in the home of Dr. George H.W. Musekamp in nearby Cheviot, Ohio. The church changed its name to Pilgrim United Church of Christ in 1960 with the merger of the Congregational Christian Churches and the Evangelical and Reformed Churches. Dr. Musekamp secured a half-acre donation from the cemetery for the 43 original members of the congregation to build their church building. In spring, 1871, the cornerstone was laid, and the building was completed using all-volunteer labor later that fall. Many of the original trustees of the cemetery, as well as many of the early lot owners of the Cemetery, were members of this church. The original church building was demolished in 1961, with the present building in use since December of that year. The church purchased the Hahn property directly west of the cemetery and made it into a parking lot in the summer of 1961. Pilgrim United Church of Christ will celebrate 150 years at this location in 2021.

A photograph of the Pilgrim United Church in 2020. This building was constructed in 1961 after the name was changed to Pilgrim United Church of Christ. The congregation will celebrate its 150th year of worship on this site in 2021. (Photo courtesy Joe Flickinger)

This 1950's photo shows the original Pilgrim United Church. Built using volunteer labor, several families also donated Creekstone for the foundation walls as well as bricks for the upper structure. The building was finished in 1871 and demolished in 1961. (Photo courtesy Green Township Historical Association)

This photo shows the back of the original building as it was being demolished in 1961. Several headstones from Bridgetown Cemetery are visible in this photo. The current Pilgrim United Church of Christ building stands in this location today. (Photo courtesy Green Township Historical Association)

Stop #5

Walking further north along the cemetery road on the right-hand side is the family plot of the George Aring Family. George Aring was a part of the original board of cemetery trustees. He and his wife Louisa held considerable amounts of land in Green Township and were involved in many land deals throughout the area. George was a Green Township Trustee, and was also a contractor in Hamilton County and is listed in many newspaper records as receiving contracts for infrastructure projects in the area. Aring's family also owned land along Race Road next to the second Bridgetown School. The cemetery was interested in purchasing this large piece of land in the early 1920s. When the cemetery trustees learned that the Bridgetown School District was interested in buying the property, they backed off pursuing the property for expansion of the Cemetery. This large stone for George and his wife used to have a large urn, draped in a veil on the top of this large marker. According to trustee minutes, the urn broke off and cracked during a large thunderstorm in the early 1970's. This symbol is "probably the most common nineteenth-century funerary symbol" meant to show the "symbol of a veil between heaven and earth."[51]

---

[51] Douglas Keister, *Stories in Stone a Field Guide to Cemetery Symbolism and Iconography* (Salt Lake City: Gibbs Smith, Publisher, 2004), 137

[54]

This photo shows the headstone of George H Aring, one of the original cemetery trustees. A stone urn draped in a veil used to sit on top of the stone. This funerary art usually represented the "veil between heaven and earth."[52] (Photo courtesy Joe Flickinger)

---

[52] Ibid, 137

[55]

Stop #6

We now visit the final resting place of Philip
Steinman I, one of the original trustees of
Bridgetown Cemetery, as well as one of the founding
members of nearby Pilgrim United Church of Christ.
Steinman, a stonemason from Neustadt, Germany,
spent many years building stone houses, barns,
bridges, culverts, stone-walled wells, and brick and
mortar cisterns around Green Township and
Cheviot. He also did chimney brickwork around
Cincinnati, as well as building walls and terraces.[53]
Steinman, who immigrated to Cincinnati in 1838,
was also one of the builders of the First German
Protestant Church(today's Pilgrim Church) as well
as the chief builder of the cemetery receiving vault
in 1877. Many of Steinman's descendants still live
in the area today.

---

[53] Phillip Steinman, *Beechwood Flats* (New York: Vantage
Press, 1960), 15

This photo shows the Steinman plot, with a stone obelisk at its center. Philip Steinman mandated in his will that a monument like this should be placed on his family plot behind the church he helped build.[54] (Photo courtesy Joe Flickinger)

[54] Ibid, 11

This undated photo shows Philip Steinman I. The photo is believed to have been taken sometime in the late 1800s. (Photo courtesy Bridgetown Cemetery Archives)

Know all Men, *That we, George H. Aring, Martin Barwick, Gerhard Stammel, Geo. H. Musekamp, Phil. Steinmann, and Phil. Boyer, former Trustees; and Geo. Aring, Jacob Wuest, Gerhard Stammel, G. H. Musekamp, Fred. Behning, and John Olenshoff, present Trustees of the First German Protestant Cemetery Association of Green Township, Hamilton County, Ohio, for, and in consideration of the sum of Twenty-five Dollars*

This image shows a portion of an 1866 deed from a family burial plot that lists Philip Steinman and the rest of the original members of the first board of trustees. Note that family lots were sold for $25 in 1866. This amount of money would have been the equivalent of around $400 today. (Bridgetown Cemetery Archives)

Stop # 7

This lot is the last resting place of additional members of the Musekamp family highlighted in one of the earlier stops on this tour. The largest headstone of Johanna is unique to the oldest section in the cemetery. This marker, made from a dark, heavy stone shows a date of death several years before the cemetery was established. According to some of the earliest cemetery records, Johanna was moved from another graveyard to Bridgetown Cemetery several years after the death of her husband in the 1870s. It was common for a spouse to be moved to another cemetery if the family desired the couple to be together, especially if the original cemetery was further away from the family. The large black stone of Johanna features a willow tree in the center, which is meant to symbolize grief and sorrow, but also everlasting life or immortality.

This was a common symbol in the 1800s on headstones.[55]

[55] Douglas Keister, *Stories in Stone a Field Guide to Cemetery Symbolism and Iconography* (Salt Lake City: Gibbs Smith, Publisher, 2004), 67

This is the headstone of Johanna Musekamp, who was the mother of George.H.W Musekamp. Her death in 1845 predated the establishment of Bridgetown Cemetery by nearly 20 years. After the death and burial of her husband in Bridgetown Cemetery in 1874, the Musekamp family had her remains moved from another cemetery to rest beside her husband. Her husband's stone also features a willow tree. (Photo courtesy Joe Flickinger)

Stop #8

We now explore the earliest section of the cemetery that is the first that opened, and which contains some of the oldest burials. This section is simply labeled "Section 1" in cemetery records and contains almost all family lots. The inscriptions on the oldest stones are written in German script, highlighting many early burials in the cemetery. These headstones were made from a white, very brittle stone that can easily crack and break. Many of these tombstones have been cracked- some have broken due to weathering, and still, others have fallen over and have been set in the ground to prevent further damage. The people buried in this section were also members of the nearby First German Protestant Church of Green Township. For many years, the cemetery would hold trustee meetings in the Sunday School Room of the church. Some of the inscriptions on the headstones in this section are also illegible due to weathering.

This picture shows the oldest section in Bridgetown Cemetery. The earliest document from this section in the cemetery archive is a deed from 1866, which shows a family lot sale for $25. (Photo courtesy Joe Flickinger)

Stop #9

This section was laid out in the early 1900s to handle a continued influx of newer residents in the early 20th century as roads improved and more modern transportation options like streetcars and automobiles began to be available to residents of the area. This section was laid out next to two houses on Nicholas Ave, which was a small dead-end street that also was home to the Sisters of St. Francis Oldenburg Convent across the street at St. Aloysius Gonzaga Roman Catholic Church. Nicholas Ave was later connected to Weirman Ave, and lost its name. Weirman Ave is named after the Weirman Family; several members of the family acted as marshals for the village of Cheviot. Marshals act as the chief of law enforcement for village governments in the state of Ohio.[56] The two houses adjoining this section were used by several sextons of the Cemetery, as well as various uses of the First German Protestant Church. According to trustee minutes, sextons dug graves and handled general maintenance in the cemetery. These houses were torn down in the 1960s for the parking lot and fellowship hall for Pilgrim United Church of Christ.

---

[56] Dave Yost, "Ohio Village Officers Handbook," *Ohio Auditors Website* (Office Auditor of the State of Ohio, March 2017), last modified March 2017, accessed July 31, 2020, https://www.ohioauditor.gov/trainings/lgoc/2017/VillageOfficer Handbook.pdf, 2-13

[65]

This section was laid out in the early 1900s to handle an influx of residents to Green Township. The Sisters of St. Francis Oldenburg Convent, seen prominently across what was then called Nicholas Ave, was built in 1953. (Photo courtesy Joe Flickinger)

The Menz Family served on the cemetery board from the late 1800s until 1985. Many family members helped shape the physical layout of the cemetery through negotiations in 1939 with the Schaeperklaus family to purchase the farm just north of the original property. This family lot includes the grave of Jacob Menz, a Civil War veteran, and a former cemetery board member. Jacob lost part of an arm in battle during the Civil War. He and his family were also prominent members of the First German Protestant Church. Jacob's relative, Reinhard Menz, who is buried nearby, was a long-serving Secretary-Treasurer of the cemetery board of trustees. The main monument on this family lot is an obelisk, which was meant to symbolize a ray of sunlight.[57] The base of this monument has fern leaves inscribed on the sides, which were meant to express humility, frankness, and sincerity.[58]

[57] Douglas Keister, *Stories in Stone a Field Guide to Cemetery Symbolism and Iconography* (Salt Lake City: Gibbs Smith, Publisher, 2004), 16

[58] Ibid, 47

The Menz Family plot features as its main monument an obelisk, which traces its roots back to ancient Egyptian architecture. Many cemeteries in the 1800's featured obelisks as representative of "rays of light." The base of this monument also features fern leaves and a monogram "M." (Photo courtesy Joe Flickinger)

This photo is of Jacob Menz, one member of the Menz family that had a long record of service to the cemetery through a volunteer position on the cemetery board of trustees. Jacob served in the Ohio Infantry during the Civil War, where after being wounded and losing his arm, he returned to live and work in Cheviot, Ohio. (Photo courtesy Menz/Morretta Family)

Buried near the Menz obelisk is Reinhard Menz, who served decades on the volunteer cemetery board of trustees as Secretary-Treasurer. Reinhard served in this capacity until he died in 1929. (Photo courtesy Mez/Morretta Family)

Stop #11

In a time before mechanical equipment, graves were dug by hand. Winter burials were difficult and the cemetery needed a place to store bodies until the weather broke. The cemetery receiving vault was built in 1876-1877 to meet that need. Stonemason and cemetery trustee Philip Steinman I oversaw the construction of this building. Cemetery records show that this receiving vault held the caskets and bodies of six individuals total in the years this building was used for this purpose. There were also two individuals whose bodies were stored here overnight, when the bodies were in transit to another cemetery. In 1880, the cemetery trustees purchased a bell from the Buckeye Bell Company in downtown Cincinnati for the steeple of the building. This bell was rung when a funeral procession entered cemetery grounds until the early 1930's when the practice was discontinued. The vault building has been used as a storage building and a historical point of interest for the original sections of the cemetery. In 2008, the remnants of Hurricane Isaac moved through the Cincinnati area, and the sustained winds from this storm caused significant damage to the building. From 2010-2012, the cemetery raised funds to rehab and replace the roof, complete necessary brickwork, and repaint the entire structure. A sign was affixed to the front of the building honoring the businesses and groups that donated to the rehabilitation of the building.

This photo from the cemetery archives is believed to be from the late 1940s. The cemetery receiving vault can be seen on the extreme left-hand side of the picture. This photo is the oldest known image of the cemetery receiving vault. (Bridgetown Cemetery Archives)

This photo shows the cemetery receiving vault in 2019 after a fresh coat of paint to give the building a sharp look as a historical centerpiece for the original sections of the cemetery. (Photo courtesy Joe Flickinger)

This 1960-61 photo was taken in front of the vault
doors, showing the view up the hill to the newly
developed sections. The administration office is not
completed, and the tributary creek, which passed
through cemetery property at the bottom of the hill
has just been filled in, but not yet graded and

seeded. (Photo courtesy Bridgetown Cemetery
Archives)

This photo, taken in early 1961, shows the original
sections of the cemetery shortly before the tributary

creek, which cut the original property off from the new property off of Harrison Ave., was filled in with a drainpipe. Fill dirt from a widening of Glenway Ave was brought in to complete the filling in of the ravine through the cemetery. The receiving vault would be in the upper right of this photo behind several trees. (Photo courtesy Dennis Kramer)

This photo showed the same view in 2017. The tributary creek, which divided the two sections of the cemetery, is now a grassy knoll. The refurbished receiving vault is pictured in the upper right. (Photo courtesy Joe Flickinger)

Stop #12

This tree-stump shaped headstone is one of the unique headstones in the original sections of the cemetery. "Treestones," or tree stumps, were popular during the mid to late 1800's, or Victorian Era. Treestones could be ordered from Sears & Roebuck catalogs, owing to their widespread use in the Midwest. Many of these unique funerary items were meant to symbolize lives cut short.[59] In this case, Helena Knierim died at the young age of 45. Located near the bottom of the stone are fern leaves, which on a treestone were meant to symbolize

---

[59] Douglas Keister, *Stories in Stone a Field Guide to Cemetery Symbolism and Iconography* (Salt Lake City: Gibbs Smith, Publisher, 2004), 65

humility, frankness, and sincerity.[60] Also surrounding the stone are ivy leaves, which expressed attachment, friendship, and undying affection. In this case, the leaves are also three-pointed, which usually indicated that it was meant as a symbol of the Trinity.[61]

[60] Ibid, 67
[61] Ibid, 57

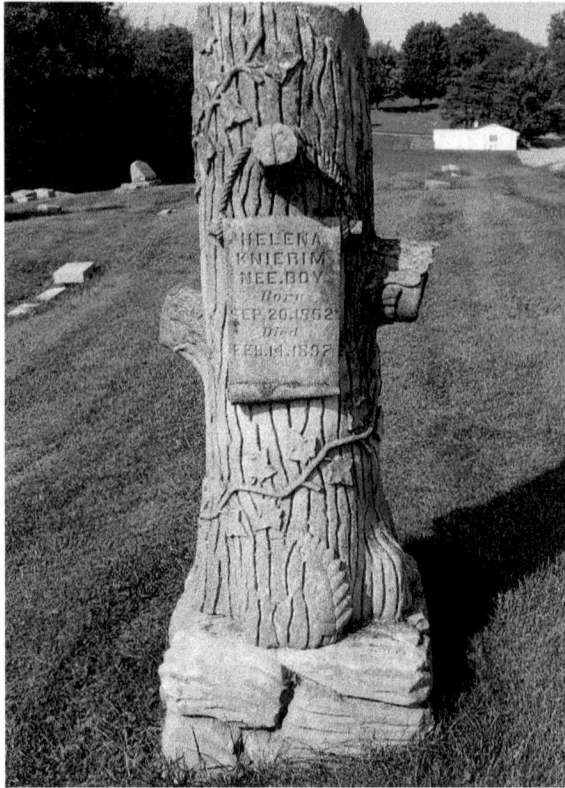

The Knierim Treestone, which is the headstone of
Phillip and Helena Knierim, rests in one of the
original sections of the cemetery.[62] These stones,
which could be purchased out of Sears & Roebuck
Catalogues, were popular funerary art when the
deceased died early in life, showing a life cut
tragically short.

---

[62] *Archives of Bridgetown Cemetery Association,* Burial Records
1875-1914

Stop #13

This stop contains the graves of several significant figures in the history of the cemetery. The Menz-Morretta family lot includes the graves of more members of the Menz family, whose years of service to the cemetery were many. These men and women helped shaped the cemetery from its time as a small rural cemetery serving mainly German Protestants immigrant families to the largest non-denominational cemetery in the area. Ed Menz was a long-time trustee who also served as Secretary-Treasurer until he died in 1968. Ed Menz also ran a very successful nursery business in the Western Hills area. Menz Lane in Green Township is named after the Menz Nursery, which stood on that land off of South Road. Ed's daughter, Carmen Menz-Morretta, served as Secretary-Treasurer from 1968 until she died in 1983. Carmen's husband, Herman "Bud" Morretta, was Bridgetown Cemetery Superintendent from 1960 to his death in 1985. He helped design, lay out, and oversee the opening of the new sections in the 1960s. Morretta helped modernize and update equipment, installed landscaping, and worked towards upgrading the roads in the cemetery until he died in 1985.

The Menz-Morretta family plot contains the graves of several family members who as members and officers of the board of trustees helped shape the look of the cemetery. Their leadership helped in development of the 12 acres of land purchased in 1939 from a farm into the longest operating and largest cemetery still serving Green Township. (Photo courtesy Joe Flickinger)

This picture shows Ed Menz, who took over as
secretary-treasurer of the volunteer cemetery board
of trustees after the death of his father, Reinhard
Menz, in 1929. In addition to serving in this
capacity until he died in 1968, Ed ran the successful

[82]

Menz Nursery, located off of South Road in Green Township. Today, the nursery site is a subdivision, with Menz Lane named after the family and nursery. (Photo courtesy Menz/Morretta Family)

This photo shows a Menz Nursery truck in the 1950s or 1960s. These trucks would have been a common sight in Bridgetown Cemetery during this time. Many of the first landscaped areas in the newly developed sections featured vegetation from Menz Nursery. (Photo courtesy Menz/Morretta Family)

This photo shows Carmen Menz-Morretta, who took over as Secretary-Treasurer of the cemetery after the death of her father, Ed Menz, in 1968. Carmen transformed the position into one that had an official office in the cemetery administration building, as well as established the first filing system for cemetery records, some of which are still used today. (Photo courtesy Menz/Morretta Family)

This picture shows Bud Morretta, who served from 1960 until his death in 1985 as Superintendent of

Bridgetown Cemetery. He was one of many who helped modernize the cemetery practice, policies, and procedures. Bud is pictured here wearing the cemetery uniform that he instituted for cemetery employees. (Photo courtesy Menz/Morretta Family)

Stop #14

Our last stop features the family monument of several members of the Ruebel family, which had a significant role in not only the history of the First German Protestant Church but also the development of the community of Bridgetown. The family at one time ran the Bridgetown Hotel at the corner of Bridgetown and Race roads. Many people today would remember the building as the Wagon Wheel Saloon. This building was torn down in 2008. The family also owned 46 acres of land at the intersection of Race and Reemlin roads. In 1871, this land provided much of the stone of the foundation of the original First German Protestant Church building. This enormous monument features an urn with a veil on top, which symbolizes the "veil between heaven and earth."[63] The memorial features the family name carved on the base, with the family members' names inscribed in the center of the monument.

---

[63] Douglas Keister, *Stories in Stone a Field Guide to Cemetery Symbolism and Iconography* (Salt Lake City: Gibbs Smith, Publisher, 2004), 137

The Ruebel Family monument is the last stop on our points of interest tour of the original cemetery. The Ruebel Family were significant contributors to the history of Green Township in the late 1800s. (Photo courtesy Joe Flickinger)

Chapter Four:
Cemetery Expansion Points of Interest

This walking tour of the expansion of Bridgetown Cemetery begins at the cemetery office located at the geographic center of the entire 22-acre cemetery property. The tour highlights points of interest on the property, which was purchased in 1939, developed through the 1950s, and officially opened in 1962. The sections in this portion of the cemetery are laid out in contrast to the original parts of the cemetery with even rows, headstone height restrictions, and limits on decorations placed on graves. This section dramatically mimics the surrounding neighborhoods which were developed in Green Township in the 1950s and 1960s suburban sprawl post-WWII where homes looked very similar to one another with nicely manicured grounds.

While the cemetery has posted speeds of 5 mph on the cemetery roads, please be aware of traffic moving through these roadways. Please respect the privacy of those visiting graves in these sections. This section of the cemetery is the most active, so please be aware of mud and other imperfections on the roadways. While the ground crews do a lot of maintenance, some roads do become covered in mud or debris, especially after a rainstorm. Cars may be parked at the marked spaces at the administration building.

Cemetery Expansion points of interest. Begin at Cemetery Office. Points of Interest begin at #1.

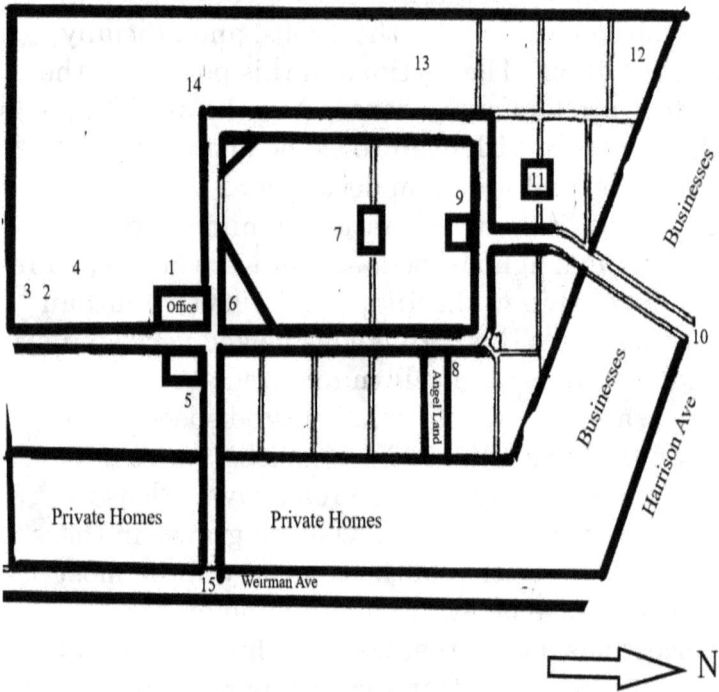

13

12

14

Businesses

11

9

7

4   1

3 2

Office

6

Businesses

10

5

8

Angel Land

Harrison Ave

Private Homes

Private Homes

15   Weirman Ave

N

Stop #1

We start this tour of the newer sections of the cemetery at the administration building. This building houses the administration offices, shop bays for the repair of equipment, and cemetery grounds maintenance equipment storage. The cemetery archives are stored in this building as well. The need for the building became apparent when the development of the newer sections necessitated more equipment, an office for storage of paperwork and records, and a place to do repairs on cemetery equipment. The office also serves as the meeting space for the cemetery trustees at least four times a year. This building was built in 1961 with volunteer labor acquired from a local bricklayers union. Men came in on Saturdays and Sundays and worked for 4-6 hours; they were treated to a lovely meal provided by the cemetery. An addition was built onto the back of the building in 1963 to accommodate more equipment.

The cemetery administration building followed the design of the cemetery to fit in with the rest of the surrounding neighborhood and it is often mistaken for a small house. In reality, it was built to resemble the neighboring houses. (Photo courtesy Joe Flickinger)

Stop #2

The Green Township Cemetery, sometimes referred to as the "Township Cemetery" in older obituaries, was initially located on the south side of Harrison Ave west of Glenmore Ave where it served the Green Township hamlet known as Cheviot. The actual documentation from the establishment of this cemetery may never be found. Although one interpretation states that in 1809, after the establishment of Green Township, the Burnet, Findlay, & Harrison Land Company set aside this plot of land to Green Township for use as a public cemetery and a meeting house/religious building, no firm documentation exists to back up this claim. The earliest known burial took place in 1812. In 1822, the deed was transferred to the newly formed Bethel Baptist Church (later renaming itself Westwood Baptist Church), which established a cemetery on the other side of Harrison Ave. The last known burial to take place in the original acreage was in 1920. Over the years, the cemetery fell into disrepair and the church sold the property to the City of Cheviot in early 1975. Cheviot decided to move the cemetery to this spot in Bridgetown Cemetery. The city paid for the remains to be moved, which occurred from May to July 1975. The single headstone is dedicated to the lives and memories of the pioneers who were buried in the cemetery. Many early township families are buried here, including John Craig, who founded Cheviot, as well as Johnsons, Stathems, and Thomas Egan, Green Township's only casualty from the Mexican War.

This gently sloping mound of earth with a single stone holds the remains of the pioneer Green Township Cemetery. Some of the pioneers who were reinterred here include John Craig, who platted out the street grid of the present-day city of Cheviot. (Photo courtesy Joe Flickinger)

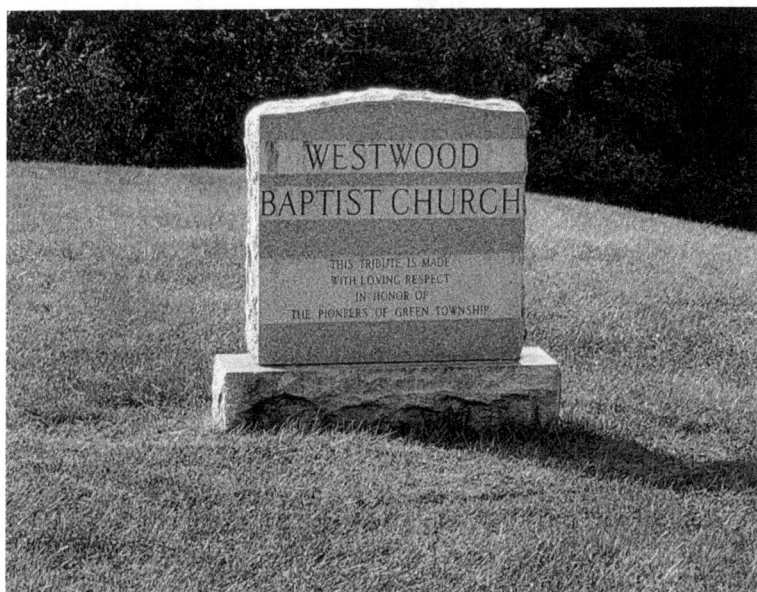

This single stone was placed on top of the reinterred
remains of the Green Township Cemetery. It reads,
"This tribute is made with loving respect in honor of
the pioneers of Green Township." Another notable
pioneer buried here is Thomas Egan, a resident of
Green Township, killed at the Battle of Monterey in
the Mexican War in 1846. Westwood Baptist Church

was the name of Bethel Baptist Church in 1976.
(Photo courtesy Joe Flickinger)

This photo dates to the 1930's, and is one of the few images of the original location of the Green Township Cemetery known to exist. (Photo courtesy Green Township Historical Association)

Stop #3

This point of interest is located next to the Green
Township Cemetery site and contains several graves
that were moved from an old family cemetery. This
cemetery was named the Frondorf Family Cemetery
in a deed that dated back to 1854. This small
cemetery, situated on less than two-hundredths of
an acre of land in between South and Fiddlers Green
roads, contained the graves of seven pioneers who
were reinterred in Bridgetown Cemetery after the
property was sold. The Probate Court ordered the
burials to be moved, and in April 1989, the seven
graves and three headstones were moved to
Bridgetown Cemetery.

These three headstones represent the graves of Stephen and Catherin Wood, Clarkson Wood, and Frances Worthington, which were moved from a small family cemetery elsewhere in Green Township in 1989. (Photo courtesy Joe Flickinger)

Stop #4

This location is one of the main reasons why it took so long for the new property to be developed after it was purchased in 1939. This unnamed tributary creek of Muddy Creek ran right through what would have been the edge of the property of the original cemetery. It prevented cars and vehicles from easy travel from the original cemetery to the newly acquired land. This tributary creek began at the border between Cheviot and Westwood. It continued through the cemetery and passed Wagon Wheel Saloon, followed Glenway Ave and then Westbourne Drive to Schaible Creek. Schaible Creek empties into Muddy Creek, which flows into the Ohio River. This natural barrier prevented the two properties from being fully connected adequately until 1963 when work was completed by Metropolitan Sewer District to enclose the creek into a large drainpipe and bury it in the ground. Fill dirt from the widening of Glenway Ave created the gently rolling grassy knoll you see today.

This gently rolling knoll of grass is all that remains of the tributary creek of Schaible Creek that cut through the two cemetery properties until 1963 when the work by Metropolitan Sewer District was completed. (Photo courtesy Joe Flickinger)

This photo shows the recently completed work on the drainpipe that buried the creek running through the middle of the cemetery. This created gently rolling fields. The above photo dates from around 1963-1965. (Photo courtesy Bridgetown Cemetery Archives)

This photo shows the view of the tributary creek from the older sections of the cemetery in 1974. The roads are recently paved, the trees are growing, and burials are beginning in the newer sections. The cemetery office is now complete, with its addition built onto the back of the building. (Photo courtesy Bridgetown Cemetery Archives)

Stop #5

This stop, right in front of the cemetery administration building, is the cemetery materials pits, built in 1975, to store materials used by the cemetery grounds crew for upkeep and maintenance of the cemetery grounds. The walls are three feet high and made from basic cinderblock. Materials such as topsoil for planting grass seed, mulch for the flower beds, and gravel for filling in low spots in the cemetery roads are stored here. During the January 1978 blizzard that hit the Cincinnati area, the cemetery stored several truckloads of sand here to provide traction on cemetery roads. In the 1980's and 1990's, the board of trustees repeatedly discussed building a roof over the materials pits, as well as potentially enclosing the area to keep the materials from washing away during heavy rains or melting snows. Due to pressing grounds maintenance needs and budgets, the project was never started.

The cemetery materials pit located directly in front
of the cemetery administration office was
constructed in 1975. (Photo courtesy Joe Flickinger)

Stop # 6

The newest garden to be established in the cemetery, the Contemplation Garden, was established in 1999. This garden features several benches meant for quiet contemplation in the bottom corner of the Garden Section of the cemetery. Several large, mature trees frame this shaded, quiet reflection area. At the center of the garden is a four-foot-high angel. This garden is a popular spot for visitors to the cemetery to stop and enjoy a quiet place to remember their loved ones or have their lunch on a beautiful day. The garden was created in 1999 with a single bench and gravel walkways. The angel was added in 2003, and additional seats were added in 2020 for multiple visitors to enjoy this spot for reflection.

This photo shows the newest garden and reflection area in Bridgetown Cemetery. Located near the cemetery administration office at the bottom of the garden section, this spot has quickly become a popular spot for visitors to the cemetery. (Photo courtesy Joe Flickinger)

[108]

Stop #7

The Garden Section of the newer sections of the cemetery features grave markers that are all level with the ground and centered around a monument modeled on an example cemetery trustees viewed at a funerary trade show in the 1950s. The monument features two planters surrounding a central upright stone. On one side, the memorial reads, "More things are wrought by prayer than this world dreams of." The other side of the upright central stone reads, "In my father's house are many mansions. If it were not so, I would have told you. I go to prepare a place for you." This monument has been a popular spot for visitors to the Garden Section since it opened for burials in 1962. Each side of the memorial features a single bench for visitors.

This photo looks south on the Garden Section monument which reads, "In my father's house are many mansions. If it were not so, I would have told you. I go to prepare a place for you." This shaded point of contemplation is a popular spot for visitors to this section. (Photo courtesy Joe Flickinger)

This photo looks north, and shows the Garden Section monument that reads, "More things are wrought by prayer than this world dreams of." This site is a popular visiting spot for quiet contemplation in the evenings when the surrounding trees shade the sun setting to the west. (Photo courtesy Joe Flickinger)

This photo shows the Garden Section monument after it had been built in the early 1960s before the addition of its central upright stone. This photo faces the south and shows the older sections of the Cemetery in the background. (Photo courtesy Bridgetown Cemetery Archives)

This photo shows the finished Garden Section monument in the mid-1960s after the central monument stone was inscribed and installed. Today, shrubbery, flowers, and grass are now familiar

sights in the cemetery. (Photo courtesy Bridgetown
Cemetery Archives)

This photo shows the area around the Garden
Section monument before installation began.
Representatives from an equipment company were
demonstrating their min-backhoe called "the little
monster" for several cemetery trustees. According to

the trustee minutes, they decided to pass on purchasing the backhoe. The trustees would not buy a backhoe until 1995. (Photo courtesy Bridgetown Cemetery Archives)

Stop #9

We now visit the infant and child section of the cemetery, known as Angel Land. According to the cemetery board minutes, a person had expressed regret that they had to bury their recently deceased child amongst the adult sections in the original portion of the cemetery. They were afraid their recently deceased child would be lost in the larger headstones of the adult sections. When designing the new part of the cemetery in the 1960s, the trustees made a special note to lay out a child and infant section so that the graves could be found easily. This section was added to the plans and featured smaller graves with smaller stones for the children buried here. A small monument at the front center of the section featuring the words Angel Land in a little nook, with a small statue featuring hands and wings cradling a small child identifies this section.

This is the central monument of the Angel Land section of the newer parts of Bridgetown Cemetery. This monument features a statue of a baby, cradled by angel wings and hands. This is the second statue for this monument; the original figure broke in a rainstorm and was replaced with this figure. (Photo courtesy Joe Flickinger)

This photo shows the Angel Land monument after it was completed in the early 1960s. Shrubs, flowers in the front planter, and newly planted sod surround the memorial. (Photo courtesy Bridgetown Cemetery Archives)

This photo shows the same area of Angel Land in the early 1970s after replanting the shrubs surrounding the Angel Monument. (Photo courtesy Bridgetown Cemetery Archives)

Stop #10

Entering Bridgetown Cemetery from Harrison Avenue brings you to the centerpiece of the cemetery. Originally a grove of bushes, this flagpole was installed in 1987 after a generous donation by Guardian Savings Bank. The landscaping has changed significantly since its installation, including the addition of benches in March 2020 thanks to an Eagle Scout Project.

The area where the current flagpole and landscaping currently stand was originally a grove of bushes surrounding several benches. Thanks to a donation by Guardian Savings Bank, this area now features a flagpole and well maintained seasonal landscaping. This photo is from November 1986. (Photo courtesy Bridgetown Cemetery Archives)

This photo is from March 1987 after work was completed on the flagpole and landscaping. For the first 30 days after the flagpole was finished, the trustees flew a flag in honor of Bud Morretta, who had passed away in 1985. (Photo courtesy Bridgetown Cemetery Archives)

This photo shows the flagpole after a landscaping refresh in 2015. In 2020, bench seating was added by a Boy Scout Eagle Scout Project to create place for reflection and quiet contemplation. (Photo courtesy Joe Flickinger)

Stop #11

This stop on the tour takes us to the stone pillars, which adorn both sides of the main entrance to the cemetery from Harrison Ave. According to the cemetery board minutes, it was arranged for a local stonemason to volunteer to build the stone pillars in 1959. The iron gates which hang on these pillars were originally used at the cemetery entrance at Bridgetown Road and had metal lettering, which said Bridgetown Protestant Cemetery. New letters were attached to the gates when the name changed to Bridgetown Cemetery acknowledging the change to a non-denominational cemetery open to all faiths. Today, the pillars feature metal signs with the new street address on one side, and the name Bridgetown Cemetery on the other. This has served as the mailing address of the Cemetery since the opening of the new sections in 1961.

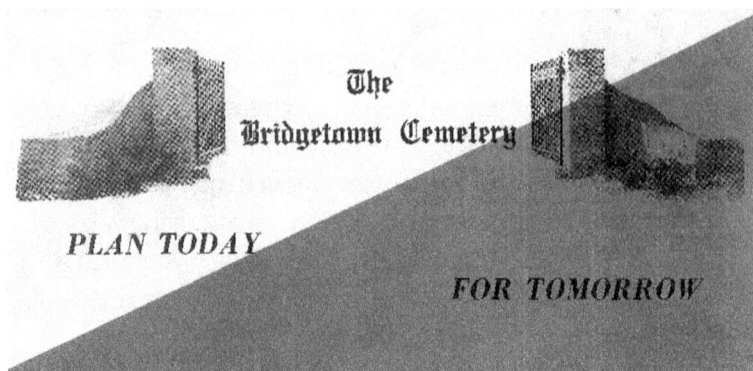

The
Bridgetown Cemetery

PLAN TODAY

FOR TOMORROW

This cemetery brochure, which was used from the newest sections opening in 1961 until the early 1970s, shows the earliest known images of the original stone pillars and iron gates. (Courtesy Bridgetown Cemetery Archives)

This picture of the main entrance of the cemetery on Harrison Avenue is from 1987. The metal signs on the stone pillars were refinished, the iron gates repainted, and the landscaping refreshed. The cemetery entrance would look this way for another 15 years when more landscaping was installed to beautify the corridor. (Photo courtesy Bridgetown Cemetery Archives)

This picture is also from 1987 and shows the reverse view of Harrison Ave from the main cemetery entrance. Notice the vacant land across from the cemetery, which is today light office and retail buildings. (Photo courtesy Bridgetown Cemetery Archives)

This photo shows the main entrance and one of the stone pillars after new flower beds were created in 1996. The iron gates were also repainted, and a brand-new mailbox was installed. (Photo courtesy Bridgetown Cemetery Archives)

This photo shows the cemetery entrance on Harrison Ave in 1999 after a massive landscape overhaul. New bushes, annuals, and fresh paint for the iron gates made the entrance look very attractive. (Photo courtesy Bridgetown Cemetery Archives)

Stop #12

This point of interest in the cemetery was the last of the significant monuments to be planned and completed. This monument, completed in the mid-1960s and inscribed with the Lord's Prayer, acts as a central focal point for the sections which back up to housing built on adjacent Raceview Road in the 1950s and 1960s. This is the final monument to be constructed, as these sections would be the last of the major sections to be laid out until the 1990s and early 2000s.

This photo shows the Lord's Prayer monument in the mid-1960s after it was completed, with the planters holding annual flowers. As with the other monuments, this memorial had bushes planted around the perimeter. These bushes were removed in the mid-1980s. (Photo courtesy Bridgetown Cemetery Archives)

This photo shows the same monument in 1987, this time with more burials and fewer bushes surrounding the monument. For reference, the large building in the background is Bridgetown Middle School of the Oak Hills School District. This section experienced sales increases through the 1980s. (Photo courtesy Bridgetown Cemetery Archives)

This photo shows the Lord's Prayer monument in 2019. The bushes, which were initially planted to surround the memorial had been long since removed. In their place, a small concrete bench has been added to provide a place for quiet reflection. (Photo courtesy Joe Flickinger)

Stop #13

We now visit a recently laid out section of the cemetery behind the Lord's Prayer monument that is to be used only for in-ground cremains. As more individuals chose cremation for themselves or their loved ones, cemetery trustees discussed adding a section to meet this growing need. Since the 1920s, the cemetery had allowed cremated remains to be buried on regular cemetery lots. Many consumers in the 21st century sought new options to bury their loved ones in a respectful but cost-effective way. These lots are all smaller than traditional burial lots and can fit two cremation containers with concrete urns and is allowed a smaller headstone. These lots are priced lower than full-size traditional lots and have attracted considerable interest. This section was laid out in June 2016 and was officially opened in November 2017.

A photograph of the new cremation section recently laid out by the cemetery grounds crew is designated for smaller lots that would hold two cremated remains. All headstones are to be smaller as well. (Photo courtesy Joe Flickinger)

Stop #14

This land is where the next sections of the cemetery will be laid out and sold. Initially, the board of trustees felt this area would be divided and used in the 1980s and 1990s. They even planned for another monument to identify this section. However, sales slowed in the later 1970s changing the need for these sections to be laid out. With urgent maintenance needs in other parts of the cemetery, trustees decided to cancel plans for a new monument. If sales and burials continue at their current pace, the cemetery predicts that these sections, which border Bridgetown Middle School, will not be needed for new burials and sales until at least the 2040s. The road through this area of the cemetery was maintained as a gravel road from its construction in 1967 until it was paved in 1995.

This photo from 1965 shows the sections that border Bridgetown Middle School. Cemetery Superintendent Bud Morretta even had his crews plant an area in the distance with bushes in preparation for a monument, which ended up not being pursued by the cemetery trustees. (Photo courtesy Bridgetown Cemetery Archives)

This photo shows the same area in 2020. The road that cuts through these sections was created as a gravel road in 1967, then was permanently paved with asphalt in 1995. The cemetery predicts that these sections will not be opened to sales until the 2040s. (Photo courtesy Joe Flickinger)

This photo from the cemetery trustee minutes shows their idea for a central monument for the sections that would border Bridgetown Middle School. The cemetery later abandoned the project for more pressing needs on the cemetery grounds. This memorial would have been similar to the Lord's Prayer memorial. (Photo courtesy Bridgetown Cemetery Archives)

Stop #14

We now visit land owned by the cemetery that may not be developed for over 50 years. This land is at a slightly lower elevation than the rest of the cemetery and is slowly being filled in with excavated dirt from other parts of the grounds. Organic materials like grass clippings, tree and bush trimmings, and fallen leaves from cemetery trees that have been mulched are placed in this area of the cemetery. A rough gravel road provides access for cemetery equipment with heavy trailers to dispose of fill dirt and other plant materials. The cemetery allows the grass on much of this property to grow to a height that is more natural.

This section of the cemetery is for fill dirt from other areas of the cemetery. This is where organic materials such as tree and bush trimmings, and mulched leaves from the fall are also disposed for compost. When grass gets too high to run the mulching mowers during the spring in some parts of the cemetery, grass clippings are left in this area as well. (Photo courtesy Joe Flickinger)

[141]

Stop #15

This point of interest represents the last stop on the tour of the newer sections of Bridgetown Cemetery. The cemetery purchased this small piece of property in 1964. Today it is currently used as the main entrance to the cemetery for funeral processions. This road features access off of Weirman Avenue, which has a lower volume of traffic than Harrison Avenue or Bridgetown Road. This entrance provides funeral processions with a safer entrance to the cemetery without fear of traffic incidents that could occur on busier roads. This road is gated and closed off to through traffic at all other times and is opened only for funerals.

This road leads to Weirman Avenue and was purchased in 1964 by Bridgetown Cemetery. It is currently used for funeral processions since Weirman Avenue has less traffic. This road is closed to through traffic. (Photo courtesy Joe Flickinger)

Appendix 1

Bridgetown Protestant Cemetery

Dedication and Consecration
of
Harrison Avenue Section

Sunday, October 1, 1961
3:00 p.m.

This is the front of the program from the opening ceremony of the new sections from 1961. (Bridgetown Cemetery Archives)

Appendix 2

Past Presidents of Bridgetown Cemetery Association
Board of Trustees

Fred Zorn
J Schmidt
Johann Miller
Andrew Engel
Jacob Wagenbach
Martin Nachtigall
John Schwander
William Wehrmeyer
Fred Schaeperklaus
Clifford Sturtz
Gilbert Letzler
Walter Schrader
Walter Stroschen
Glenn Haubrock
Ronald Scheidt
William Flickinger

***Note: This list is incomplete, and only represents the names of past presidents going back to 1890. Trustee meeting minutes were hand-written in a very hard to read German script called "Kurrent." Names of presidents of the board of trustees were not always written in trustee minute books before 1910 in legible handwriting. No board minutes remain from 1864-1884.

Appendix 3

Cemetery Sextons/Superintendents

Charles Kinnemeyer 1919-1934
William Spreen, 1934-1960
Herman "Bud" Morretta, 1960-1985
Stanley Stall, 1985-1994
Lou Stroschen, 1994-1998
John Scheidt, 1998-2002
Daniel Herzog, 2002-present

***Note: This list is also incomplete. The job of sexton(head of ground maintenance/digging graves) and who filled that role was not recorded in cemetery trustee meeting minutes until Charles Kinnemeyer was appointed in 1919.

Appendix 4

<u>Secretary/Treasurer of the Board of Trustees</u>

G. Stammel
Jacob Menz
Reinhard Menz
Ed Menz
Carmen Menz-Morretta
Verna Carney
Judy Boeshart
Mary Scheidt

***Note: This list begins in 1890 with G. Stammel.
Like many of the board minutes, these were hand-
written in German script called "Kurrent" and not
easy to understand or read.

Appendix 5

This photo shows Stanley Stall, who became
Cemetery Superintendent in 1985 after the death of
longtime Superintendent Herman "Bud" Morretta.
Stall oversaw continued improvement projects,
including roads, equipment, and the flagpole
monument. Stall retired in 1994 but stayed on part-
time until 1998 to help with sales as well as funerals

when needed. Stall fully retired in 1998. (Photo courtesy Bridgetown Cemetery Archives)

Appendix 6

This photo shows Cemetery Superintendent Lou Stroschen(left) and part-time groundskeeper Joe Flickinger (right) working on the new fencing being installed in one of the older sections in spring 1997. Stroschen helped institute the use of the cemetery's backhoe in 1995, which allowed the cemetery to dig

its graves without using an outside contractor.
(Photo courtesy Bridgetown Cemetery Archive)

Appendix 7

This photo shows longtime groundskeeper Jeff
Dreigon fixing damage to the grass along the side of
the road from car tires in November 1987. This
work is quite common for the cemetery ground
crews. When cars pull along the side of the roadway,
and it has rained, it is easy for tires to leave

indentations in the ground that need to be fixed. (Photo courtesy Bridgetown Cemetery Archives)

Bibliography

Primary Sources

Archives of Bridgetown Cemetery Association. July 2000. Items from History of Bridgetown Cemetery, Formerly Known as The First German Protestant Cemetery of Green Township, Administration Building, Cincinnati, Ohio.

—Board of Trustees Meeting minutes, 1938-1961, Box 1

—Board of Trustees Minute Book, 1961-1995, Box 1

—Board of Trustees Minute Book, 1998-2010, Box 1

—Burial Records 1875-1914, Box 1

—Cemetery Burial Records, 1875-1932, Box 1

—Cemetery Burial Records, 1965-1978, Box 1

—Cemetery Dedication and Consecration Program, Box 3

—Constitution and Bylaws of the First German Protestant Cemetery Association, 1910, Box 3

—Dedication Brochure, Box 2

—Incorporation Certificate, 1897, Box 2

—Recorders Deed Book Copy, 1865, Box 2

[153]

Deed Book of Hamilton County, Deed Book of Hamilton County, Hamilton County Recorder's Office (Cincinnati, OH, n.d.)

Secondary Sources

Dickore, Marie. *"The Cheviot, Ohio Cemetery." Bulletin of the Historical and Philosophical Society of Ohio*, first ser., 14 (January 1956).

Flickinger, Joe. *A Bicentennial History of Green Township: Uncovering a Jewel in the Crown of the Queen City; 1809-2009*. Westminster, Maryland: Heritage Books, 2011.

Green Township Webpage, (accessed 4/29/2020) http://www.greentwp.org

Heglin,William. "Honor to the Dead," *The Cincinnati Daily Enquirer* (Cincinnati, July 3, 1847)

Keister, Douglas. *Stories in Stone a Field: Guide to Cemetery Symbolism and Iconography*. Salt Lake City: Gibbs Smith, Publisher, 2004.

Knepper, Dr. George, *The Official Ohio Lands Book*, Columbus Ohio, Auditor of the State of Ohio Publication, 2002

Kramb, Edwin A. *Buckeye Battlefields*. Springboro, OH: Valhalla Press, 2006

Leuders, Jeffrey, *Pilgrim United Church of Christ, 1870-1990* (Cincinnati, OH: Church Printing, 1990).

Looker, Palmer & Reynolds, ed., "On Tuesday Last," *Liberty Hall*, (Cincinnati, December 22, 1812)

Long, Alexander, "Green Township History for Harvest Home Picnic," *Cincinnati Daily Enquirer* (Cincinnati, August 27, 1869).

Ruffing, Paul. *St. Aloysius Gonzaga 150th Anniversary Booklet, 1866-2016.* Cincinnati, Ohio: St. Aloysius Gonzaga Church, 2016.

Remler, Mary H., ed. Hamilton County, Ohio, Burial Records, Volume 10: Green Township. Vol. 10. Westminster, Maryland: Heritage Books, 2012

Scully, Henry, ed, *Remember When...Monfort Heights*, Cincinnati Ohio, Monfort Heights Civic Association, 1977

Silberstein, Iola, *Cincinnati, Then and Now*, Cincinnati, League of Women Voters, 1982

Steigerwald, Shauna. "Scout Spruces up Cemetery for Eagle Project." *Cincinnati Enquirer*. Cincinnati, June 6, 2009, sec. Hometown Section

Suburban Topics "Bulldozer Unearths Casket," *Cincinnati Enquirer* (Cincinnati, May 16, 1975), sec. Metro Section

Steinman III, Phillip, *Beechwood Flats*, New York NY, Vantage Press, 1960

Tolzmann, Don Heinrich, *German Heritage Guide to the Greater Cincinnati Area,* Milford Ohio, Little Miami Publishing, 2003

Yost, Dave. "Ohio Village Officers Handbook." *Ohio Auditors Website.* Office of the Auditor of the State of Ohio, March 2017. Accessed July 31, 2020. https://www.ohioauditor.gov/trainings/lgoc/2017/VillageOfficerHandbook.pdf

Index

About the Author

Joe Flickinger is a lifelong resident of the Cincinnati area. Joe holds a B.A. in History and an M.Ed in Educational Administration from Xavier University, and has also completed an M.A. in History with a concentration in Public History from Southern New Hampshire University. Joe has worked as a history teacher in Cincinnati for over 20 years. He serves as Vice-President of the Green Township Historical Association and is a member of the Coleraine Historical Society. Joe maintains professional memberships in the American Historical Association, National Council of History Education, Organization of American Historians, National Council on Public History, and the American Association for State and Local History. Joe's other books include *A Bicentennial History of Green Township; Uncovering a Jewel in the Crown of the Queen City,1809-2009*, released in 2011, and 2018's *A History of Colerain Township: From Frontier Wilderness to Suburban Sprawl*. He is married to his wonderful wife Kathleen and has three beautiful children.